S0-AWG-952

THE ART OF WAR

THE ART OF WAR

THE ART OF WAR

Including the translated
THE SAYINGS OF WU TZU

SUN TZU

With an Introduction by
TOM BUTLER-BOWDON

CAPSTONE

This edition first published by Capstone Publishing 2010

Introduction copyright © Tom Butler-Bowdon, 2010

The material for *The Art of War* and *The Sayings of Wu Tzu* is based on the complete 1908 edition of *The Book of War: The Military Classic of The Far East*, translated by Captain E. F. Calthrop, R.F.A, published by John Murray, Albemarle Street, London, and now in the public domain. This edition is not sponsored or endorsed by, or otherwise affiliated with Everard Calthrop, his family or heirs.

Registered office
Capstone Publishing Ltd. (A Wiley Company), The Atrium, Southern Gate, Chichester, West Sussex, PO19 8SQ, United Kingdom

For details of our global editorial offices, for customer services and for information about how to apply for permission to reuse the copyright material in this book please see our website at www.wiley.com.

Reprinted August 2010, December 2010, February 2011, December 2011, September 2012, July 2013, January 2014, September 2014, March 2015, September 2015, December 2015

All rights reserved. No part of this publication may be reproduced, stored in a retrieval system, or transmitted, in any form or by any means, electronic, mechanical, photocopying, recording or otherwise, except as permitted by the UK Copyright, Designs and Patents Act 1988, without the prior permission of the publisher.

Wiley also publishes its books in a variety of electronic formats. Some content that appears in print may not be available in electronic books.

Designations used by companies to distinguish their products are often claimed as trademarks. All brand names and product names used in this book are trade names, service marks, trademarks or registered trademarks of their respective owners. The publisher is not associated with any product or vendor mentioned in this book. This publication is designed to provide accurate and authoritative information in regard to the subject matter covered. It is sold on the understanding that the publisher is not engaged in rendering professional services. If professional advice or other expert assistance is required, the services of a competent professional should be sought.

Library of Congress Cataloguing-in-Publication Data
9780857080097
A catalogue record for this book is available from the British Library.

Set in 11/15pt, NewBaskerville-Roman by Thomson Digital, India
Printed in the United Kingdom by TJ International Ltd., Padstow

CONTENTS

CONTENTS

FOREWORD

Sun Tzu's book, *The Art of War*, has appeal throughout the ages because business feels like warfare. We wish romantically that it were not so, but the daily lives of workers and executives alike are full of emotional traumas not unlike those that soldiers face at war.

A successful executive and a friend of mine used to work at a *Fortune 500* company. Shortly after he had retired, he confided in me: "I *put up* with them (his former employer) for 37 years." A client of mine worked at his non-profit for several decades and, when he retired, he moved as far away from his former employer as he could.

It is no wonder that I bought and read this ancient Chinese classic shortly after I resigned from my *Fortune 500* company job as a manager in international sales and marketing in the spring of 1983. My corporate job had given me so much angst and dissatisfaction I had cinematographic visions of large-scale warfare that felt like the apocalypse in my dreams. I wanted to set up my own business. I wanted to have control over my own fate. I knew I must read Sun Tzu in order to survive in this do-or-die, cut-and-thrust world of business.

One of the early stories in Sun Tzu that fascinated me was the way he handled the unruly concubines of his client, the Duke of Wu. He beheaded those who didn't take his training seriously, and succeeded in turning court ladies into fearsome warriors. War is serious and unsentimental, just like the forces at work in the marketplace. To fail to obey good judgment is fatal. I took this lesson to heart.

After 15 years of practicing my craft in helping companies promote and sell American-made products and services in the China market, I ran up against the most feared moment of my consultancy. My most important client did not get any business from China for one full year, and my annual retainer was about to be renewed. It was late December and I was about to meet my client. I had served my client for 14 years by that time. We trusted each other and we did not feel we had to play "games" with each other. I was telling myself that perhaps I should tell my client to drop me because I couldn't foresee when the China market would pick up. I was tempted to commit professional suicide.

I was fortunate that the same evening when I was thinking such thoughts, my lawyer friend Mariann invited me to her house for dinner. I told Mariann my dilemma and she said: "James, it is not up to you how your client wants to use you and your service. See your client tomorrow and stay quiet. Listen to what they say to you first.''

As I sat in front of my client the next morning, I obeyed Mariann's advice because it was so Sun-Tzu-esque. I controlled my feelings of insecurity. I did not become defensive or belligerent. Most importantly, I did not initiate a ''fight'' with my client on whether or not I am worthy of their retainer.

Miraculously, as I sat in silence while keeping my poise, my client told me in a matter-of-fact manner that they wanted to renew my contract. Not only that, they wanted to give me a three-year (not the usual one-year) contract. In addition, my client raised my consulting fee for me. I was speechless. I said: ''Thank you.'' The ''negotiation'' session took no more than five minutes.

This story is related to Sun Tzu because I put into practice the most important principle – and the ultimate goal – of the spirit of *The Art of War,* namely, the greatest victory is one that does not require fighting a war.

My client's strategy proved to be correct. They understood the business cycle in their industry. They wanted to retain me in anticipation of doing battle with our competitors. In less than two years, the China market picked up and they succeeded beyond their expectations. It is hard enough to battle with one's competitors; it is fatal to fight an unnecessary war with one's benefactor.

Sun Tzu tells us not to do battle unless it is really necessary. This is just one of the many pieces of timeless advice in the book that you are about to read.

James Chan, PhD
President, Asia Marketing and Management
Philadelphia, USA
Author of *Spare Room Tycoon*
www.AsiaMarketingManagement.com
www.SpareRoomTycoon.com

AN INTRODUCTION
BY TOM BUTLER-BOWDON

That a person of today, a civilian, would want to read a manual for waging war that is over two thousand years old must say something about that work's enduring power.

But what, exactly, can the modern reader get from *The Art of War*?

First, in the capitalist knowledge society we live in, in which individual qualities are quickly exposed, the book's emphasis on the importance of personal character and knowledge as the keys to success has never been more relevant. Its author, Sun Tzu, insisted that wise generals or leaders could not simply rely on their knowledge of the terrain or the capabilities of the opposition, but had to know themselves. To become invincible, they first had to develop deep understanding, and full control, of their own reactions, to be the same in the face of praise or blame. Victory, Sun Tzu says, comes to those who have developed an ethic of constant refinement and improvement. It is never possible to control other people, but by developing our own strength of character, knowledge and insight we can build invincibility. In Chinese philosophy, leadership *is* character. People with great character, developed over time, naturally become leaders.[1]

Secondly, *The Art of War* is intriguing because of its spiritual underpinnings. While other military treatises from its era, and indeed modern war manuals such as Von Clausewitz's *On War* and the US Marines' *Warfighting*[2], are simply technical manuals on the mechanics of waging war, *The Art of War* provides a whole philosophy for action that applies to life as much as battle.

"In war there is no fixity," Sun Tzu says. The wise general does not simply come up with a plan and rigidly follow it, but is attuned to the "Tao" of a situation, or the particular way events are moving at any one moment. Such a leader can act objectively and with perfect timing.

SUN TZU AND HIS IMPACT

Constant fighting between feudal states and dynasties, plus the need to defend borders from invaders (the Great Wall had been built long before Rome began its spread into northern Europe), gave China ancient experience in war strategy and methods. Amid a rich heritage of military annals, histories and manuals stands *Sunzi Bingfa* (*The Art of War*).

Both it and *Wuzi*, or *Sayings of Wutzu* (see Part II of this volume), are included in *Seven Military Classics*, the canon of war manuals first collated in 11th-century China.

The Art of War came into being when Sun Tzu was asked by the king of Wu, Ho Lu, to compose a work encapsulating his warrior wisdom. Sun Tzu, or Sun Wu as he is also known, was a real person. Born around 544 BCE, a native of the Qi state (now Shandong province), he was a contemporary of Confucius during the "Spring and Autumn" period when northern China was essentially a collection of warring states. His father had been a general and his grandfather a provincial governor. By his early 30s he had became known as a brilliant military strategist, leading the armies of Wu (the smallest of 13 states at the time) to great victories. Such "masters of war," translator EF Calthrop notes, "were in no sense patriots but professional strategists, continually changing their employer." Yet this very independence and objectivity were the source of their wisdom and prowess.

The impact of *The Art of War* on warfare in China could be compared to that of Machiavelli's *The Prince* on politics in Europe and the West. The Chinese king Qin Shi Huang, for instance, adopted the book's principles to unite China, and centuries later Chairman Mao would use it for a similar purpose.

Its influence transcends its original time and place. The *Sonshi* (or Sun Tzu), as it is known in Japan, was brought there as early as the 8th century, and later played an important role in Japan's unification. It was reputedly core reading for Napoleon in his European conquests, and in more recent times, American generals Douglas MacArthur and Norman Schwarzkopf, along with the Vietnamese general Vo Nguyen Giap, noted their debt to the book. It remains on the syllabus in military colleges around the world.

This is the case even though, until little more than a century ago, in the West *The Art of War* was little known.

THE TEXT

First communicated orally, over time Sun Tzu's original tenets were made into a book, complemented by commentary and annotations from other military philosophers including Li Quan, Du Mu, Mei Sheng-yu, and the great warlord Cao Cao. For a period, doubt was cast on whether Sun Tzu was actually the author of *The Art of War*, with some scholars arguing that it was simply an aggregation of the philosophies of various military leaders, or the work of Sun Tzu's descendant Sun Bin. However in 1972, in Shandong, bamboo-strip versions of *The Art of War* and *Sun Bin's The Art of War* were found in a Han dynasty (206 BCE–220CE) tomb, confirming each as separate works and Sun Tzu as the author of the text long attributed to him.

The first European translation was completed in 1782 by a French Jesuit priest living in China, Joseph Amiot, but it was another 120 years before the first English translation appeared. Captain Everard Ferguson ("EF") Calthrop was a British officer who had served in the Boer War before being stationed with the Foreign Service in Japan. As part of its then alliance with Japan, Britain deemed it useful for 50 or 60 of its officers to learn Japanese and study their host country's military system. Calthrop was exposed to the *Sonshi* and learned of its impact on the history of Japanese military strategy.

Calthrop's first translation of the *Sonshi* was published in 1905 in Tokyo, before it was fully revised for British publication in 1908 under the title *The Book of War: The Military Classics of the Far East*. This version carries well the basic force of Sun Tzu's maxims and, along with his translation of the *Sayings of Wutzu*, Calthrop's translation[3,4] forms the basis of this Capstone edition.

In Calthrop's wake, Lionel Giles, a sinologist and keeper of Far East antiquities at the British Museum, published his own translation[5]. In it, perhaps resenting the incursion of a mere army officer onto his academic turf, he trenchantly criticized Calthrop for various perceived omissions and mistakes, and for lack of scholarship. However, as historian and military scholar Hamish Ion[6] has noted, Calthrop was unfairly maligned since his translation was based on a Japanese version of Sun Tzu, which would always have differed from a Chinese text. Moreover, it was never Calthrop's purpose to provide exhaustive scholarly commentary, but rather to mine the wisdom of Sun Tzu for his higher-ups in the British Army, showing how that institution could be reformed and illuminating how Japan could have defeated Russia in the Russo-Japanese war[7].

After the Calthrop–Giles era many other translations of *The Art of War* followed, including Samuel Griffith's notable work of 1963, and they keep coming. Recent versions[8] tend to emphasize the book as a guide to managing any kind of conflict, positing Sun Tzu as an enlightened Taoist master.

Below is a brief exploration of some of the main concepts in the work as we can apply them to work and life today.

Some versions begin with an account provided by the Chinese historian, Ssu-ma Ch'ien, of Sun Tzu's notorious actions at the court of King Ho Lu. Though not included in the main text, this apocryphal event is also discussed below.

In its basic form, *The Art of War* consists of Sun Tzu's 13 chapters, beginning with "Preliminary Reckoning," or the preparation for war, and ending with "The Employment of Spies." Yet modern readers should not expect a neat sequence of lessons. This is, after all, an ancient and sometimes enigmatic text that works best when we let it seep into our consciousness over several readings.

THE WAY OF THE WISE LEADER

The five factors

Sun Tzu identified "five indispensable matters" that had to inform a leader's decisions: The Way, Heaven, Earth, Leader, and Law. What do these actually mean, and how can we apply them in our own context?

In Sun Tzu's army, **The Way** refers to the extent to which there is singularity of purpose, with leader and soldiers tightly bound to the same goals. There is very little such a body of people cannot accomplish, since they move with the power and purpose of one. The obvious lesson for organizations of any place or time: Do not waste energy on internal divisions, and move ahead united.

Related to the individual, The Way involves the five virtues of humanity, righteousness, propriety, wisdom, and faith, suggesting a mature person who, having developed themselves over many years, is "all of a piece" and galvanized by clear goals.

Heaven and **Earth**, as Sun Tzu uses the terms, are the conditions within which a general wages war. In a modern context, this can be interpreted as heightened, present-moment awareness of the social, political and economic environment in which one lives and works. Such awareness allows one to make the most of opportunities, avoid dangers, and develop intuition about what is to come.

Leader means a person or an organization that exhibits timeless values. The combination of "hard" and "soft" attributes – Sun Tzu specifically refers to sincerity, wisdom, benevolence, courage, and strictness as qualities of the great general – marks out an individual as deeply humane, and yet someone who means business. An organization, similarly, must be seen to be tightly focused on its mission, and yet always be acting ethically.

Law in Sun Tzu's terms refers to "the ordering and partition of troops." For ourselves, we can take it to mean having one's house in order and establishing priorities. In an organization, Law may mean the appointment of the right people, who know exactly what they are accountable for and who have the resources to execute their mission.

Of these five factors of action, Sun Tzu says, "to know them is to conquer; to know them not is to be defeated."

Taking whole

Sun Tzu notes the great costs and evils of war, particularly prolonged wars, and so reserves his greatest praise for the general who is able to avert battle in the first place, who can "subdue the enemy without fighting."

However, if preventing conflict is not possible, the next greatest skill is to "take whole," or achieve victory with the minimum loss to life and property. Such a leader "causes the enemy's forces to yield, but without fighting; he captures his fortress, but without besieging it; and without lengthy fighting takes the enemy's kingdom." The key is to build up momentum, then strike hard and either conquer or get away quickly. The wise general works continually to channel his soldiers' combined energies into a single powerful force that can achieve this. "Like the well-judged flight of the falcon, in a flash crushing its quarry, so should the stroke be timed," says Sun Tzu.

A clean victory will also involve giving the enemy an honorable exit strategy. When your forces begin to surround the enemy, Sun Tzu counsels, "allow him an outlet" through which escape is possible. If you push him into a corner with no chance of retreat it will cost you, as he will fight with the desperation of one who has nothing to lose.

Planning and preparedness

"Taking whole," as opposed to the shattering of a foreign kingdom through brute force, can be achieved. But it requires brilliant strategy and timing, great forethought, planning, and knowledge.

The wise leader never leaps into battle as an emotional response, but plans exhaustively to ensure that his positions will be impregnable, while identifying the weaknesses in the enemy.

Of Sun Tzu's "five occasions when victory can be foretold," number four is:

When the state is prepared, and chooses the enemy's unguarded moment for attack.

It is always a mistake to rely on assumptions about the enemy's positions and plans. Real confidence comes from knowing that your own positions are unassailable, and only then deciding to go into battle.

Sun Tzu says never to engage a force that is your equal. You must be certain of your superiority before the first arrow is shot. You must not only have greater numbers and better equipment, but be tactically superior, more nimble, have better information, and possess greater unity of purpose. "Skilful soldiers," Sun Tzu notes, "make defeat impossible."

In hindsight, the victor is always seen to be the one who made the most calculations prior to conflict. By practicing the way things may go, we are much less put off course by a change of events in the heat of battle.

"If the condition of both sides with regard to these matters be known," Sun Tzu says in relation to preparation and readiness, "I can foretell the victor."

Self-knowledge and field knowledge

With lessons for today, Sun Tzu warns darkly of protracted wars that drain a state's resources and sap the people's energies. These are generally the result of two things: overconfidence about one's forces (a problem of self-knowledge); and information about a foreign country (deficiencies in terrain knowledge).

And yet, Sun Tzu observes:

> He who knows both sides has nothing to fear in a hundred fights.

We all know people who seem to know everything about their subject or profession or business, yet do not advance because of personal flaws or, worse, lack of awareness of them. Among the "dangerous faults" of a general, Sun Tzu lists: impetuosity or recklessness, which leads to death; over-cautiousness or cowardice, which leads to capture; quick temper, easily provoked by insults; and rigid propriety or sense of honor, in which the threat of shame leads to bad decisions. Any of these traits can lead to the loss of a critical battle or war. If a general has not got mastered his destructive traits before entering the theater of war, or is not even aware of them, it is a travesty of his position.

The lesson: In our own lives, the work of self-examination and self-control is essential to real success. In life, as in war, we need *both* self-knowledge and field knowledge to win.

Regarding the latter, to do really well in any area we need to add to our knowledge of it continually, and to be aware of daily changes and developments, to "know the terrain." Sun Tzu constantly harps on the importance of the various conditions and grounds of battle. For us, this means continually analyzing the changing environment and conditions in our field of work, obtaining as much data as possible before committing our resources.

Mastery of information

As we try to make our knowledge as perfect as possible, we must work to give the opposition the wrong picture of us. Deception or pretense, Sun Tzu famously says, is at the heart of warfare.

The opposition should never know of your real strengths and capacities. In any negotiations, as in war itself, our hand is always stronger when the other side thinks we have more resources than we actually do, or thinks we are weaker than we really are. This will make it arrogant and therefore vulnerable to unexpected attack.

Similarly, by pretending to be in disorder, we can surprise the enemy with the force of our attack at the right moment. When we are far away from the field of battle, we must somehow make the enemy think we are close, and vice versa. Generally, when the assumptions the other side has about us are wrong, we are stronger. Hence Sun Tzu's emphasis on the importance of spies (see Chapter XIII) in obtaining correct information.

The larger view and timing

Number one of Sun Tzu's "five occasions when victory can be foretold" is this:

When the general knows the time to fight and when not to fight.

The wise leader is able to see the whole of a situation and read the way things are moving. This provides the genius of timing. The opposite of this is to cling on to particular course of action regardless of conditions. This is the hallmark of an ideologue, but on the actual battleground it is a terrible approach. *The Art of War* warns never to act according to beliefs or dogma but in light of the information flowing in a particular moment. Moreover, we must always challenge conventional wisdom in order to arrive at the truth of a situation.

It comes as no surprise that General Norman Schwarzkopf, considered one of the best generals in modern times and vital to the successful defeat of Saddam's invasion of Kuwait, is a fan of Sun Tzu. As the Chinese warrior predicted of a great general, Schwarzkopf was not a rigid ideologue, but strategized according to opportunity and conditions. In contrast, the relative failure of America's second war with Iraq has widely been put down to a disastrous combination of blind idealism and poor knowledge of the insurgency. To the extent that US forces employed "shock and awe" at the start of battle, they followed Sun Tzu's teachings; but as Sun Tzu points out, brute force alone may not be enough. To be wily, to surprise and deceive, yet to act in a detached way and without arrogance, are all qualities crucial to victory.

Regarding detachment, Sun Tzu observes:

> *War should not be undertaken because the lord is in a moment of passion. The general must not fight because there is anger in his heart.*

The passions may change, he notes, but "a country, once overturned, cannot be restored; the dead cannot be brought to life."

Managing people

On this subject, it is worth recounting the rather gruesome story of Sun Tzu's service to Ho Lu, the King of Wu, which prefaces some versions of *The Art of War*.

Ho Lu had just read Sun Tzu's 13 chapters and was keen to see if his ideas could be applied universally. With Sun Tzu's assurance that they could, the king asked, "Women, too?", and Sun Tzu answered, "Yes." Ho Lu duly asked for the 180 women who lived in his palace to be brought outside, where it was agreed that Sun Tzu would train them in military drill.

Sun Tzu divided them into two companies, and though they seemed intelligent, the girls did not take the exercise too seriously and were soon in fits of laughter at the manly drill they were asked to perform. He tried to give more orders, but there was no discipline in the ranks. At this point, Sun Tzu gravely stated, "If words of command are not clear and distinct, the general is to blame. But if his orders are clear, and the soldiers nevertheless disobey, then it is the fault of their officers."

At this, he ordered the leaders of each company, the king's favorite young concubines, to be beheaded. The shocked king tried to protest, but Sun Tzu refused, noting that he had been commissioned to train the king's forces as he saw fit, and was simply carrying out that charge.

Sun Tzu took the next women in line and made them the platoon leaders. This time, however, the fearful women performed the drill perfectly and without a sound.

Sun Tzu then informed the king that his "soldiers" were ready for action, and would do anything asked of them. The awestruck Ho Lu appointed Sun Tzu as his general, and he went on to win many great victories for his client.

Sun Tzu's approach to "managing people" may be brutal, but it challenges us to see that a clear and strong line of command can create a loyal and motivated force capable of anything. Number three of Sun Tzu's five predictors of victory is:

When government and people are of one mind.

To achieve this, you need authority.

As already noted, Sun Tzu taught that the most successful armies act as if they are one body. Time is saved and energy is preserved when all parts of the body act in unison, with a single directed energy. A similar *esprit de corps* is the holy grail of today's organizational leaders, but without resorting to beheading, how can we achieve Sun Tzu's level of unity and loyalty? Jack Welch, who very successfully ran the huge General Electric company, famously believed that you could do it through a system of "kicks and hugs"[9]. This sounds much softer than what is advocated in *The Art of War*, and yet Sun Tzu himself points out the need for rewards as well as threats in handling people:

> *They who are the first to lay their hands on more than ten of the enemy's chariots should be rewarded.*

He notes that soldiers must always be treated with humanity, which in turn produces obedience. Through this combination, Sun says, "we obtain victory."

His approach to managing people, and indeed his advice on how the wise leader must conduct themselves, can be summed up in one sentence from Chapter 11:

> *The general should be calm, inscrutable, just and prudent.*

Sun Tzu identifies "over-solicitude" with his staff to be a flaw in a general. Alfred Sloan, the legendary head of General Motors, would have concurred. Sloan felt the need to remain somewhat aloof from his managers, as this gave him objectivity in his decision making. And in a way that may shock some of today's managers who mistakenly feel they have to remain "best mates" with their subordinates, Sloan observed (in Sun Tzu fashion) that you don't have to like your staff members. What matters is that they perform[10].

Sun Tzu provides some further advice:

> *Orders should direct the soldiers; but while what is advantageous should be made known, what is disadvantageous should be concealed.*

In other words, give orders but don't give reasons for them, and relate only good news. For today's managers, so used to making information as freely available as possible within the organization, this will seem a paranoid reaction. And yet, in war it is the sensible thing to do, since the more your forces know, the greater the chance that this knowledge will be uncovered by the enemy. Furthermore, this policy of "keep them guessing" can make a modern workforce more geared to loyal, unified action instead of going through a democratic charade involving endless meetings and discussions. At the same time, it can prevent costly leaks to the competition or the press.

Overall, Sun Tzu notes, the aim of the general is "to lead his army as a man leads another by the hand." On occasion, this can mean placing them in challenging, even harmful situations. Yet the leader does this for their own good and the good of the group, for desperation brings out the best in people.

Finding opportunities

In military strategy, Sun Tzu warns, "to besiege [the enemy's] citadel is the worst expedient." Attacking great strongholds will bring great loss of life and material costs to one's army, yet with its reserves of men and materials, and high-walled impenetrability, such an attack may barely dent the enemy.

The warning could not be more relevant today. In business terms, we should think twice before launching ourselves at a market dominated by a huge, deep-pocketed single company or cabal. In career terms, it is foolhardy to believe we will succeed in a field where success would be costly and a long time in coming, if at all.

The Sun Tzu way, in battle and in life, is to find opportunities where, taking account of your resources, you will have the most impact. Only sometimes will this involve going at the enemy head on. More often it requires thorough calculations that ensure you identify the ground on which you will be strongest. Sun Tzu puts it simply:

> If we attack those positions which the enemy has not defended, we invariably take them.

Going "where the enemy is not" and taking its territory is the total opposite of the "attacking walled cities and citadels" approach, and dramatically increases the likelihood of victory. If you do actually have to engage the enemy, Sun Tzu says, do so at points where it is not well defended, or attack flanks of its army that never expected to be hit.

In 2004, a book called Blue Ocean Strategy[11] became a bestseller on the basis of its seemingly novel idea that business success comes not from competing head on with the major players in the big markets, but pioneering new, highly profitable niches. This first involved intensive research of where there were untapped markets, then creating a product or service to meet them. In almost every respect, the book follows Sun Tzu's principles of "taking the enemy where it is not" – or, better still, seizing territory where there is simply no opposition to begin with.

FINAL WORD

While most of us will never find ourselves in a real battle situation, we all need strategies to operate effectively in work, love, and life, we need to be able to manage conflict, and we have to be skilled at dealing with people. *The Art of War* is a time-tested resource for "victory" in each of these areas.

The basis of Sun Tzu's teaching on strategy is that it must continually evolve, taking into account new information. This ability to take in the present moment, combined with great preparedness and unity of purpose, leads to an accurate picture of what is going on. Within this wholeness of vision, when opportunities come along they can be seized, delivering decisive wins.

As Sun Tzu powerfully suggests, the best way to approach conflict is objectively, taking account of the aims of all parties in a situation. Though this will go against the "fight for your life" mentality you may be used to, the result may be a better outcome for all with minimal losses. Furthermore, as Sun Tzu suggests, it is possible to develop one's conflict skills to such an extent that goals are achieved without even having to fight. Sun Tzu's great skill was motivating and managing people. Alongside study of the "nine types of ground" and the array of military tactics at a general's disposal, he identified study of "the hearts of men" (or the laws of human nature) as fundamental to the great leader's rise.

Though not everyone has read *The Art of War*, today's most successful individuals and organizations tend naturally to express its truths. Consider as an example of good conflict and people management a modern "general" of the business world, Warren Buffett. In his biography of the billionaire investor, Richard Lowenstein[12] recounts an episode in which Buffett chose to cooperate fully with Treasury investigators when they decided to investigate Salomon Brothers, a firm in which he held a large stake. Lowenstein describes Buffett's approach:

> *Instinctively, he shrank from confronting his adversaries, but he was superb at winning them*

*over without a fight. He did not so much con-
vince; he disarmed, he co-opted.*

Just as Sun-Tzu might have predicted, this approach led to an outcome favorable for all.

In the arenas of negotiation, conflict resolution, courtroom strategy, business strategy, "positioning" of products in marketing, political campaigning (Lee Atwater, the Republican strategist, traveled with the book), and of course military strategy itself, *The Art of War* continues to be influential. In 2007 Robert Gates, US Defense Secretary under Presidents Bush and Obama, twice referred to the strategies of Sun Tzu in testimony before Congress, and in 2009 Jia Qinglin, China's top political adviser, urged the study of *The Art of War* as a means to solving global conflicts. In business, Larry Ellison, billionaire founder of computer firm Oracle, is fond of quoting the work, as is his protégé, Salesforce.com founder Marc Benioff[13]. In sport, successful coaches and managers from soccer's Felipe Scolari, to American football's Bill Belichick and Steve Spurrier, to Australian cricket's John Buchanan and rugby's Eddie O'Sullivan, have all noted their debt to Sun Tzu's maxims.

A summary of traits follows that, if adopted, can turn you also into a wise leader known for creating brilliant outcomes. See if the thoughts and stratagems of an ancient warrior can positively have an impact on *your* life.

Tom Butler-Bowdon, 2010

THE WISE LEADER

- Controls the form of engagement, instead of reacting to it.
- Seeks to take whole, rather than seeking to destroy.
- Makes sure of victory before taking the first action, ensuring their forces are invincible.
- Lets the enemy wear itself out trying to get advantage, then lets its own force throw it off balance.
- Decides on victory, rather than wishing for it.
- Seeks to run their organization as one piece and with one spirit.
- Acts with sincerity, wisdom, benevolence, courage, and strictness.
- In the eyes of subordinates, is calm, inscrutable, just, and prudent.
- Moves quietly and without arrogance, in order to achieve the objective.
- Is a master of uncertainty and chaos, reading the flow of events in any given moment.

- Is predictable in some things, so as to be able to surprise in others.
- Is practiced in the art of deception, letting the enemy see only what they want it to see.
- Insistently seeks knowledge about the other side.
- Constantly works to increase self-knowledge.
- Continually studies human nature.

NOTES

1. As Donald G Krause noted in *The Art of War For Executives* (Penguin, 1995).

2. *On War* (1832), by Prussian general Carl von Clausewitz; *Warfighting: The US Marine Corps Book of Strategy* (US Marine Corps Staff, 1989).

3. Lieutenant-Colonel Calthrop rose to the position of British military attaché in Tokyo at the start of the First World War, before being stationed in France. He was killed in action at Ypres, France, in December 1915, still only 39, while in charge of the 38th Brigade Royal Field Artillery.

4. Calthrop's translation is presented largely intact, with some minor updating of antiquated language (e.g., "wherefore" to "therefore"). Most of his footnotes are also reproduced.

5. The full Giles translation, along with his copious commentary and notes, can be read online at Gutenberg.org. Search for "The Art of War."

6. Hamish Ion, "Something new under the Sun: E. F. Calthrop and the art of war," *Japan Forum*, 2 (1): 29–41, 1990. Ion is Professor of History at the Royal Military College of Canada, Ontario.

7. As Hamish Ion notes (p. 37), ''The carnage and siege warfare of the Western Front showed that British military strategists did not make use of Sun Tzu's ideas.''

8. See, for example, the Denma Translation Group's *The Art of War* (Shambhala, 2001)..

9. Jack Welch, *Jack: Straight from the Gut* (Warner, 2001).

10. As recounted by Peter F Drucker in *Management Cases* (HarperCollins, 1977).

11. W Chan Kim & Rene Mauborgne, *Blue Ocean Strategy: How To Create Uncontested Market Space and Make Competition Irrelevant* (Harvard Business School, 2005).

12. Richard Lowenstein, *Buffett: The Making of an American Capitalist* (Random House, 1995).

13. According to Thomas Huynh of *Art of War* website Sonshi.com, who interviewed Benioff.

KEY

Footnotes marked in *italics* are additional comments from the author. All other footnotes remain as referenced in Calthrop's original edition of *The Book of War*.

ABOUT TOM BUTLER-BOWDON

Tom Butler-Bowdon is the author of five best selling books on the classic writings in the self-help and motivational field. He has been described by *USA Today* as 'a true scholar of this type of literature'.

His first book, *50 Self-Help Classics*, won the 2004 Benjamin Franklin Award and received endorsements from personal development guru Stephen R. Covey and Harvard University's Ellen Langer. The equally successful *50 Success Classics* followed, looking at the landmark works in motivation and leadership from Napoleon Hill to Nelson Mandela. Tom's third book, *50 Spiritual Classics*, provides commentaries on some of the famous writings and authors in personal awakening, from Mother Teresa to Carl Jung to Eckhart Tolle. The two most recent additions to the series are *50 Psychology Classics* (2007) and *50 Prosperity Classics* (2008). The series has been translated into 21 languages.

Tom is a graduate of the London School of Economics and the University of Sydney, and lives in Oxford, England. His website Butler-Bowdon.com has an array of free self-development resources.

- Readers can receive a free *Art of War* bonus by sending emailing Tom@Butler-Bowdon.com with 'Art of War' in the title bar.
- See also Capstone's editions of *Think and Grow Rich*, the classic motivational text by Napoleon Hill, and *The Science of Getting Rich* by Wallace Wattles, both of which contain Introductions by Tom Butler-Bowdon.

PART 1

PART I

THE ART OF WAR

THE ART OF WAR

CONTENTS

1

PRELIMINARY RECKONING

The words of Sun the Master:

To all nations War is a great matter.
Upon the army death or life depend: it is
the means of the existence or destruction
of the State.

Therefore it must be diligently studied.

Now, in war, besides stratagem and
the situation, there are five indispensable
matters. The first is called The Way[1];
the second, Heaven; the third Earth; the
fourth, the Leader; the fifth, Law.

The Way or the proper conduct of man.
If the ruling authority be upright, the
people are united: fearless of danger, their
lives are at the service of their Lord.[2]

---

[1] The five virtues of humanity, righteousness, propriety, wisdom
and faith are known as The Way.

[2] *Their ruler or sovereign.*

Heaven. Yin and Yang[3]; heat and
cold; time and season.

Earth. Distance; nature; extent;
strategic position.

The Leader. Intelligence; truth;
benevolence; courage and strictness.

Law. Partition and ordering of troops.

These things must be known by the
leader: to know them is to conquer; to
know them not is to be defeated.

Further, with regard to these and the
following seven matters, the condition of
the enemy must be compared with our own.

The seven matters are:

The virtue of the prince; the ability
of the general; natural advantages; the

---

[3] The Yin and Yang are the two principles into which natural
phenomena are divided in Chinese philosophy. Yin is the
masculine, active, or light principle, and Yang is the feminine,
passive, or dark principle. In this connection, day and night,
rain, mist and wind are designated.

discipline of the armies; the strength of
the soldiers; training of the soldiers;
justice both in reward and punishment.

Knowing these things, I can foretell the
victor.

If a general under me fight according
to my plans, he always conquers, and I
continue to employ him; if he differ from
my plans, he will be defeated and dismissed
from my service.

Therefore, with regard to the foregoing,
considering that with us lies the advantage,
and the generals agreeing, we create a
situation which promises victory; but as
the moment and method cannot be fixed
beforehand, the plan must be modified
according to circumstances.

War is a thing of pretence: therefore,
when capable of action, we pretend
disability; when near to the enemy, we
pretend to be far; when far away, we
pretend to be near.

Allure the enemy by giving him a small
advantage. Confuse and capture him. If
there be defects, give an appearance of
perfection, and awe the enemy. Pretend
to be strong, and so cause the enemy to
avoid you. Make him angry, and confuse
his plans. Pretend to be inferior, and
cause him to despise you. If he have
superabundance of strength, tire him out;
if united, make divisions in his camp.
Attack weak points, and appear in unexpected places.

These are the secrets of the successful
strategist, therefore they must not be made
known beforehand.

At the reckoning in the Sanctuary before
fighting, victory is to the side that excels
in the foregoing matters. They that have
many of these will conquer; they that
have few will not conquer; hopeless,
indeed, are they that have none.

If the condition of both sides with regard
to these matters be known, I can foretell
the victor.

11

OPERATIONS OF WAR

Sun the Master said:

Now the requirements of war are such
that we need a thousand light chariots with
four horses each; a thousand leather-covered
chariots, and one hundred thousand armoured
men; and we must send supplies to distant
fields. The cost at home and in
the field, the entertainment of guests, glue
and lacquer for repairs, and necessities for
the upkeep of wagons and armour are such
that in one day a thousand pieces of gold
are spent. With that amount a force of
one hundred thousand men can be raised:
you have the instruments of victory.

But, even if victorious, if the operations
long continue, and the soldiers' ardour decreases,
the weapons become worn, and, if
a siege be undertaken, strength disappears.

Again, if the war last long, the country's
means do not suffice. Then, when the
soldiers are worn out, weapons blunted,
strength gone and funds spent, neighbouring
princes arise and attack that weakened

country. At such a time the wisest man
cannot mend the matter.

For, while quick accomplishment has been
known to give the victory to the unskilful,
the skilful general has never gained
advantage from lengthy operations.

In fact, there never has been a country
which has benefited from a prolonged war.

He who does not know the evils of war
will not reap advantage thereby. He who
is skilful in war does not make a second
levy, does not load his supply wagons thrice.

War material and arms we obtain from
home, but food sufficient for the army's
needs can be taken from the enemy.

The cost of supplying the army in distant
fields is the chief drain on the resources of
a state: if the war be distant, the citizens
are impoverished.

In the neighbourhood of an army prices
are high, and so the money of the soldiers

and followers is used up. Likewise the state funds are exhausted, and frequent levies must be made; the strength of the army is dissipated, money is spent, the citizen's home swept bare: in all, seven-tenths of his income is forfeited. Again, as regards State property, chariots are broken, horses worn out, armour and helmet, arrow and bow, spear, shield, pike and fighting tower, wagon and oxen used and gone, so that six-tenths of the Government's income is spent.

Therefore the intelligent general strives to feed on the enemy; one bale of the enemy's rice counts as twenty from our own wagons; one bundle of the enemy's forage is better than twenty of our own.

Incitement must be given to vanquish the enemy.

They who take advantage of the enemy should be rewarded.

They who are the first to lay their hands on more than ten of the enemy's chariots should be rewarded; the enemy's standard on the chariots exchanged for our own; the captured chariots mixed with our own chariots and taken into use.

The accompanying warriors must be treated well, so that, while the enemy is beaten, our side increases in strength.

Now the object of war is victory; not lengthy operations, even skilfully conducted.

The good general is the lord of the people's lives, the guardian of the country's welfare.

III

THE ATTACK BY
STRATAGEM

Sun the Master said:

Now by the laws of war, better than
defeating a country by fire and the sword,
is to take it without strife.

Better to capture the enemy's army intact
than to overcome it after fierce resistance.

Better to capture the "Lu" the "Tsu"
or the "Wu" whole,[1] than to destroy them
in battle.

To fight and conquer one hundred times
is not the perfection of attainment, for the
supreme art is to subdue the enemy without
fighting.

Therefore the most skilful warrior outwits
the enemy by superior stratagem; the
next in merit prevents the enemy from
uniting his forces; next to him is he who
engages the enemy's army; while to besiege
his citadel is the worst expedient.

---

[1] The Chinese army consisted of 12,500, the "lu" of 500, "tsu" of
50, and the "wu" of 6 men.

A siege should not be undertaken if it
can possibly be avoided. For, before a
siege can be commenced, three months are
required for the construction of stages,
battering-rams and siege engines; then a
further three months are required in front
of the citadel, in order to make the
"Chuyin."[2] When the general is
angered, and his patience exhausted, his men
surge like ants against the ramparts before
the time is ripe, and one-third of them are
killed to no purpose. Such are the misfortunes
that sieges entail.

Therefore the master of war causes the
enemy's forces to yield, but without fighting;
he captures his fortress, but without
besieging it; and without lengthy fighting
takes the enemy's kingdom. Without tarnishing
his weapons he gains the complete
advantage.

---

[2] The "Chuyin" was a large tower or work constructed to give
command over the interior of the enemy's fortress. High poles
were also erected from the top of which archers, each encased in
an arrow-proof box and raised by a rope and pulley, shot at the
besieged.

This is the assault by stratagem.

By the rules of war, if ten times as strong
as the enemy, surround him; with five
times his strength, attack; with double his
numbers, divide. If equal in strength,
exert to the utmost, and fight; if inferior
in numbers, manoeuvre and await the
opportunity; if altogether inferior, offer no
chance of battle. A determined stand by inferior
numbers can only lead to capture by
the enemy.

The general is the country's support. If
his aid be entire, the country is of necessity
strong; if it be at all deficient, then is the
country weak.

Now a prince may embarrass his army in
three ways, namely:

Ignorant that the army in the field should
not advance, to order it to go forward; or,
ignorant that the army should not retreat,
order it to retire.

This is to tie the army as with a string.

Ignorant of military affairs, to rule the armies in the same way as the state.

This is to perplex the soldiers.

Ignorant of the situation of the army, to settle its dispositions.

This is to fill the soldiers with distrust.

If the army be perplexed and distrustful, then dangers from neighbouring princes[3] arise. The army is confounded, and offered up to the enemy.

There are five occasions when victory can be foretold:

When the general knows the time to fight and when not to fight; or understands when to employ large or small numbers; when government and people are of one

---

[3] *Rulers or heads of state, as opposed to the general himself who is commissioned to head the army.*

mind; when the state is prepared, and
chooses the enemy's unguarded moment for
attack; when the general possesses ability,
and is not interfered with by his prince.

These five things are the heralds of
victory.

It has been said before that he who
knows both sides has nothing to fear in a
hundred fights; he who is ignorant of the
enemy, and fixes his eyes only on his
own side, conquers, and the next time is
defeated; he who not only is ignorant of
the enemy, but also of his own resources,
is invariably defeated.

IV

THE ORDER OF BATTLE

Sun the Master said:

The ancient masters of war first made
their armies invincible, then waited until
the adversary could with certainty be
defeated.

The causes of defeat come from within;
victory is born in the enemy's camp.

Skilful soldiers make defeat impossible,
and further render the enemy incapable
of victory.

But, as it is written, the conditions
necessary for victory may be present,
but they cannot always be obtained.

If victory be unattainable, we stand
on the defensive; if victory be sure, we
attack.

Deficiency compels defence;
superabundance permits attack.

The skilful in defence crouch, hidden
in the deepest shades; the skilful in attack

push to the topmost heaven.[1]

If these precepts be observed, victory is certain.

A victory, even if popularly proclaimed as such by the common folk, may not be a true success. To win in fight, and for the kingdom to say "Well done," does not mark the summit of attainment. To lift an autumn fleece[2] is no proof of strength; the eyes that only see the sun and moon are not the eagle's; to hear the thunder is no great thing.

As has been said before, the able warrior gains the victory without desperate and bloody engagements, and wins thereby no reputation for wisdom or brave deeds. To fight is to win, for he attacks only when the enemy has sown the seeds of defeat.

---

[1] Literally 9th heaven and 9th earth. The Chinese divided the earth and sky each into 9 strata.

[2] An animal's coat is thinnest in autumn.

Moreover, the skilful soldier in a secure position does not let pass the moment when the enemy should be attacked.

The army that conquers makes certain of victory, and then seeks battle.

The army destined to defeat, fights, trusting that chance may bring success to its arms.

The skilful leader is steadfast in the "Way"; upholds the Law, and thereby controls the issue.

Touching the laws of war, it is said: first, the rule; second, the measure; third, the tables; fourth, the scales; fifth, the foretelling of victory.

For the rule is the survey of land; the measure tells the amount of that land's produce; the tables its population; from the scales their weight or quality is made known; and then can we calculate victory or defeat.

The army that conquers as against the army destined to defeat, is as a beam against a feather in the scales. The attack of conquering forces is as the outburst of long-pent-up waters into sunken valleys.

Such are the orders of battle.

V

THE SPIRIT OF THE TROOPS

Sun the Master said:

The control of large numbers is possible,
and like unto that of small numbers, if we
subdivide them.

By means of drum, bell and flag,[1] the
direction of large forces in battle is possible,
and like unto the direction of small forces.

By the skilful interchange of normal and
abnormal manoeuvres are the armies certainly
preserved from defeat.

The enemy is crushed, like the fall of a
grindstone upon an egg, by knowledge of
his strength and weakness, and by the
employment of truth and artifice.

---

[1] The drum was used to beat the assembly and in the advance,
the bell as a signal to halt. Flags were of two kinds, signalling flags
and distinguishing banners.

Moreover, in battle the enemy is engaged
with the normal and defeated by the
abnormal force.[2]

The abnormal force, skilfully handled,
is like the heaven and earth, eternal;
as the tides and the flow of rivers, unceasing;
like the sun and moon, for ever interchanging;
coming and passing, as the seasons.

There are five notes; but by combinations,
innumerable harmonies are produced.
There are but five colours; but if we mix
them, the shades are infinite. There are
five tastes, but if we mix them there
are more flavours than the palate can
distinguish.[3]

In war there are but two forces, the
normal and the abnormal; but they are

---

[2] The normal and the abnormal refer to what in modern phrase
are termed the frontal or holding force and the flanking or
surprise force. *That is, a wise general engages one part of his army head
on with the enemy, while the other part moves around to surprise and
defeat the enemy.*

[3] The five cardinal tastes are acridity, bitterness, sourness,
sweetness and saline taste.

capable of infinite variation. Their mutual
interchange is like a wheel, having neither
beginning or end. They are a mystery
that none can penetrate.

As the rush of rock-shouldering torrents,
so is the spirit of the troops.

Like the well-judged flight of the falcon,
in a flash crushing its quarry, so should the
stroke be timed.

Therefore the spirit of the good fighter
is terrifying, his occasions sudden; like the
stretched cross-bow, whose string is released
at the touch of the trigger – In the maze and
tumult of the battle, there is no confusion;
in the thick of action the battle array is
impenetrable.

If discipline be perfect, disorder can be
simulated; if truly bold, we can feign fear;
if really strong, we can feign weakness.

We simulate disorder by subdivision;
fear, by spirit; weakness, by battle formation.

We set the enemy in motion by adopting different
formations to which he must conform.

If we offer the enemy a point of
advantage, he will certainly take it: we
give him an advantage, set him in motion
and then fall upon him.

The good fighter seeks victory
from spirit, and does not depend entirely
upon the skill of his men. He is careful
in his choice, and leaves the rest to battle
force; yet, when an opening or advantage
shows, he pushes it to its limits.

As a log or rock which, motionless on
flat ground, yet moves with ever-increasing
force when set on an incline, so await the
opportunity, and so act when the opportunity
arrives.

If the general be skilful, the spirit of his
troops is as the impetus of a round stone
rolled from the top of a high mountain.

VI

EMPTINESS AND STRENGTH

Sun the Master said:

To be the first in the field, and there to
await the enemy, is to husband strength.

To be late, and hurrying to advance to
meet the foe, is exhausting.

The good fighter contrives to make the
enemy approach; he does not allow himself
to be beguiled by the enemy.

By offering an apparent advantage, he
induces the enemy to take up a position
that will cause his defeat; he plants
obstructions to dissuade him from acting in
such a way as to threaten his own dispositions.

If the enemy be at rest in comfortable
quarters, harass him; if he be living in
plenty, cut off his supplies; if sitting
composedly awaiting attack, cause him to
move.

This may be done by appearing where
the enemy is not, and assaulting unexpected
points.

If we go where the enemy is not, we may
go a thousand leagues without exhaustion.

If we attack those positions which the
enemy has not defended, we invariably take
them: but on the defence we must be
strong, even where we are not likely to
be attacked.

Against those skilful in attack, the enemy
does not know where to defend: against
those skilful in defence, the enemy does
not know where to attack.

Now the secrets of the art of offence are
not to be easily apprehended, as a certain
shape or noise can be understood, of the
senses; but when these secrets are once
learnt, the enemy is mastered.

We attack, and the enemy cannot resist,
because we attack his insufficiency; we
retire, and the enemy cannot pursue,
because we retire too quickly.

Again, when we are anxious to fight, but
the enemy is serenely secure behind high

walls and deep moats; we attack some
such other place that he must certainly
come out to relieve.

When we do not want to fight, we
occupy an unfortified line; and prevent the
enemy from attacking by keeping him in
suspense.

By making feints, and causing the enemy
to be uncertain as to our movements, we
unite, whilst he must divide.

We become one body; the enemy being
separated into ten parts. We attack the
divided ten with the united one. We are
many, the enemy is few, and in superiority
of numbers there is economy of strength.

The place selected for attack must be
kept secret. If the enemy know not
where he will be attacked, he must prepare
in every quarter, and so be everywhere
weak.

If the enemy strengthen his front, he
must weaken his rear; if he strengthen

his right, his left is weakened; and if he strengthen his left, his right is weakened.

Everywhere to make preparations, is to be everywhere weak. The enemy is weakened by his extended preparations, and we gain in strength.

Having decided on the place and day of attack, though the enemy be a hundred leagues away, we can defeat him.

If the ground and occasion be not known, the front cannot help the rear; the left cannot support the right, nor the right the left, nor the rear the front. For on occasion, the parts of the army are two score leagues apart, while a distance of four or five leagues is comparatively close.

The soldiers of Wu are less than the soldiers of Yueh[1]; but as superiority in numbers does not of necessity bring victory, I say, then, that we may obtain the victory.

---

[1] Sun Tzu was a native of Wu. The kingdoms of Wu and Yueh were continually at war.

If the enemy be many in number, prevent him from taking advantage of his superiority, and ascertain his plan of operations. Provoke the enemy and discover the state of his troops; feint and discover the strength of his position. Flap the wings, and unmask his sufficiency or insufficiency. By constant feints and excursions, we may produce on the enemy an impression of intangibility, which neither spies nor art can dispel.

The general makes his plans in accordance with the dispositions of the enemy, and puts his hosts in motion; but the multitude cannot appreciate the general's intention; they see the signs of victory, but they cannot discover the means.

If a victory be gained by a certain stratagem, do not repeat it. Vary the stratagem according to circumstances.

An army may be likened to water.

Water leaves dry the high places, and seeks the hollows. An army turns from strength and attacks emptiness.

The flow of water is regulated by the shape of the ground; victory is gained by acting in accordance with the state of the enemy.

The shape of water is indeterminate; likewise the spirit of war is not fixed.

The leader who changes his tactics in accordance with his adversary, and thereby controls the issue, may be called the God of war.

Among the five elements[2] there is no settled precedence; the four seasons come and go; the days are long and short; and the moon waxes and wanes. So in war there is no fixity.

---

[2] Wood, fire, earth, metal and water.

VII

BATTLE TACTICS

Sun the Master said:

For the most part, military procedure
is as follows:

The general receives orders from his
lord; assembles and settles harmony
among the forces, and takes the field.

There is nothing more difficult than
Battle Tactics. Their difficulty lies in the
calculation of time and distance, and the
reversal of misfortune.

To make the enemy take a circuitous
route by a show of gain, and then, whilst
starting after him, to arrive before him, is
to be a master of the art of manoeuvre.

The operations of an army may reap
advantage; the wrangles of a multitude
are fraught with peril.[1]

Employing our whole force at one time
in order to gain advantage over the enemy,

---

[1] *Meaning, a general can achieve things with a good army, and will
achieve nothing, or cause great harm, with an undisciplined rabble.*

we may not have time enough to gain our object. If we push on with a portion of the force only, the transport is lost. Discarding helmet and armour; stopping neither day nor night; marching double distance; doing double work; and finally contending with the enemy at a distance of a hundred leagues: results in the loss of the general. Since the strong men arrive first, and the tired drop in rear, only one-tenth of the forces is available.[2]

A forced march of fifty leagues to secure an advantage may result in failure to the leader of the vanguard, for only half his men will arrive.

After a forced march of thirty leagues to secure an advantage, only two-thirds of the army will be available.

Further, a lack of ammunition, of supplies, or of stores, may lead to disaster.

---

[2] *Though tempting to send out ahead smaller, more mobile units of your army, this is very costly. Ultimately it is better to keep your forces together.*

The ruler who is ignorant of the designs
of neighbouring princes, cannot treat with
them.

He who is ignorant of mountain and
forest, defile[3] and marsh, cannot lead an army.

He who does not employ a guide, cannot
gain advantage from the ground.

Disguise your movements; await a favourable
opportunity; divide or unite according
to circumstance.

Let your attack be swift as the wind;
your march calm like the forest[4]; your
occupation devastating as fire. In defence,
as a mountain rests firm; like darkness
impenetrable to the enemy. Let your movements
be swift as the lightning.

Let as many as possible take part in the
plunder: distribute the profit from the
captured territory.

---

[3] *Narrow passages between mountains.*

[4] This passage was written on the standard *[personal flag]* of
Takeda Shingen, one of Japan's most famous generals.

So he who understands the crooked and the straight way conquers.

These are the methods of Battle Tactics.

According to the ancient books on war, the drum and bell are used, because the voice does not carry; the flag is used to assist the sight. The use of bell, drum, banner and flag is to attract the united attention of eye and ear.

When all are united, the strong are not left to go forward alone, the cowardly are not free to retreat unrestricted. In this way can a multitude be used.

Therefore in night fighting, beacons and drums are largely used; in day fighting, a great number of banners and flags and the enemy's eyes and ears are confounded.

We thus awe his army, and defeat his general's ambition.

In the morning the spirits are keen; at midday there is a laziness; in the evening

a desire to return. Therefore, he who
uses his soldiers well, avoids the time when
the enemy's spirits are keen; but attacks the enemy
when he is languid or seeking his camp.

Thus should the nature of energy be
turned to account.

To oppose confusion with order, clamour
with quiet, is to have the heart under
control.

To await an enemy from a distance, to
oppose hunger with satiety, rest with fatigue,
is the way to husband strength.

Do not attack where lines of banners
wave, nor the serried ranks of battle spread,
but patiently await your time.

Do not attack an enemy on high ground,
nor one who has high ground at his back.
Do not pursue an enemy who is imitating
flight; do not attack a spirited enemy.

If the enemy offer an allurement, do
not take it.

Do not interfere with an enemy who has
struck camp, and is about to retire. When
surrounding an enemy, allow him an outlet.
Do not press a desperate enemy.

These are the methods of employing troops.

VIII

THE NINE CHANGES

Sun the Master said:

In general, the procedure of war is:
the Leader, having received orders from
his lord, assembles the armies.

Do not camp on marshy or low-lying
ground; enter into friendly relations with
neighbouring states; do not linger in a far
country; use stratagem in mountainous and
wooded country; on death ground, fight.

There are always roads that must be
avoided; forces that must not be attacked;
castles that must not be besieged; ground
that must not be chosen for encounter;
orders from the lord that must not be
obeyed.

The general who knows the Nine Changes[1]
understands the use of troops; on the contrary,

---

[1] *The Nine Changes can also be interpreted as the Nine Variations, or the changeable factors that a wise general must be aware of and use to his advantage. Careful readers will note that there are in fact ten factors listed in the preceding two paragraphs. While Calthrop does not explain this, in his translation Lionel Giles refers to a note by historical Art of War commentator Wang Hsia, to the effect that "nine" is symbolic of an "indefinitely large number." Sun Tzu himself elsewhere notes that the variations in conditions faced by a general are innumerable.*

he who does not understand them can
make no use of his topographical knowledge.

In the management of armies, if the art
of the Nine Changes be understood, a knowledge
of the Five Advantages is of no avail.

The wise man considers well both advantage
and disadvantage. He sees a way out
of adversity, and on the day of victory to
danger is not blind.

In reducing an enemy to submission,
inflict all possible damage upon him; make
him undertake useless adventures; also
make neighbouring rulers move as you
would desire them by tempting them with
gain.

Therefore in the conduct of war do not
depend on the enemy's not coming, but
rely on your own preparations; do not
count on the enemy not attacking your
fortress, but leave nothing undefended.

Generals must be on their guard against
these five dangerous faults:

Blind impetuosity, which leads to death.

Over-cautiousness, which leads to capture.

Quick temper, which brings insult.

A too rigid propriety, which invites
disgrace.

Over-regard for the troops, which causes
inconvenience.

These five faults in the leader are disastrous
in war. The overthrow of the army
and the slaughter of the general arise from
them. Therefore they must be carefully
considered.

IX

MOVEMENT OF TROOPS

Sun the Master said:

Regarding the disposal of troops and observation of the enemy in relation to mountain warfare:

Cross mountains and camp in valleys, selecting positions of safety.

Place the army on high ground, and avoid an enemy in high places.

In relation to water:

After crossing waters, pass on immediately to a distance. When the enemy is crossing a stream, do not meet and engage him in the waters, but strike when half his force has passed over. Do not advance on an enemy near water, but place the army on high ground, and in safety.

Do not fight when the enemy is between the army and the source of the river.

With regard to marshes:

Cross salty marshes quickly; do not linger
near them.

If by chance compelled to fight in the
neighbourhood of a marsh, seek a place
where there is water and grass, and trees in
plenty in the rear.

In open country place the army in a convenient
place with rising ground in the right
rear; so that while in front lies death, behind
there is safety.

Such is war in flat country.

Huangti,[1] by observing these things, gained
the victory over four Princes.

As a rule, the soldiers prefer high ground
to low. They prefer sunny places to those
the sun does not reach.

---

[1] *Huang-ti (c.259–c.210 BCE) was the first Emperor of China, who
destroyed the existing feudal structure and created a centralized
administration based on 36 provinces. As heir himself to the feudal state
of Chin, on becoming Emperor he established (briefly) his Chin dynasty.
The name China derives from this.*

If the health of the troops be considered,
and they are encamped on high and sunny
ground, diseases will be avoided, and victory
made certain.

If there be rising ground, encamp on its
sunny side and in front of it; for thereby
the soldiers are benefited, and the ground
used to our advantage.

If, owing to rains in the upper reaches,
the river become turbulent, do not cross
until the waters have quieted.

Steep and impassable valleys; well-like
places; confined places; tangled impenetrable
ground; swamps and bogs; narrow
passages with pitfalls: quickly pass from
these, and approach them not. Cause the
enemy to approach near to them, but
keep yourself from these places; face
them, so that the enemy has them in his
rear.

If there be near to the army, precipices,
ponds, meres,[2] reeds and rushes, or thick

---

[2] *Lake or pond.*

forests and trees, search them thoroughly.
These are places where the enemy is likely
to be in ambush.

When the enemy is close, but quiet, he is
strong in reliance on natural defences.

If the enemy challenge to fight from afar,
he wishes you to advance.

If the enemy be encamped in open
country, it is with some special object in
view.

Movement among the trees shows that
the enemy is advancing. Broken branches
and trodden grass, as of the passing of a
large host, must be regarded with suspicion.

The rising of birds shows an ambush.

Startled beasts show that the enemy is
stealthily approaching from several sides.

High, straight spurts of dust betoken
that chariots are coming.

Long, low masses of dust show the
coming of infantry.

Here and there, thin and high columns
of dust are signs that firewood and fodder
are being collected.

Small clouds of dust moving to and fro
are signs that the enemy is preparing to
encamp for a short time.

Busy preparations and smooth words
show that the enemy is about to advance
to attack.

Big words, and the spurring forward of
horsemen, are signs that the enemy is about
to retire.

An advance of the light chariots to the
flanks of the camp is a sign that the enemy
is coming forth to fight.

Without consultation, suddenly to desire
an armistice, is a mark of ulterior design.

The passing to and fro of messengers,
and the forming up of troops, show that the
enemy has some movement on foot.

An advance, followed by sudden retirement,
is a lure to attack.

When the enemy use their weapons to
rest upon, they are hungry.

If the drawers of water drink at the river,
the enemy is suffering from thirst.

Disregard of booty that lies ready at hand
is a sign of exhaustion.

The clustering of birds round a position
shows that it is unoccupied.

Voices calling in the night betoken alarm.

Disorder in the army is a sign that the
general is disregarded.

A changing about of flags and banners
is a sign that the army is unsettled.

If the officers be angry, it is because the
soldiers are tired, and slow to obey.

The killing of horses for food shows that
the enemy is short of provisions.

When the cooking-pots are hung up on
the wall and the soldiers turn not in again,
the enemy is at an end of his resources.

Exceeding graciousness and familiarity
on the part of the general show that he
has lost the confidence of the soldiers.

Frequent rewards show that discipline is
at an end.

Frequent punishments are a sign that the
general is in difficulties.

The general who first blusters, and then
is obsequious, is without perception.

He who offers apologies and hostages
is anxious for a truce.

When both sides, eager for a fight, face
each other for a considerable time, neither

advancing nor retiring, the occasion requires
the utmost vigilance and circumspection.

Numbers are no certain mark of strength.

Even if incapable of a headlong assault,
if the forces be united, and the enemy's
condition ascertained, victory is possible.

He who without taking thought makes
light of the enemy is certain to be captured.

If a general who is strange[3] to the troops
punishes them, they cease to obey him. If
they are not obedient, they cannot be
usefully employed.

If the troops know the general, but are not
affected by his punishments, they are useless.

By humane treatment we obtain obedience;
authority brings uniformity. Thus
we obtain victory.

---

[3] *That is, has not formed an attachment.*

If the people have been trained in obedience from the beginning, they respect their leader's commands.

If the people be not early trained to obedience, they do not respect their leader's commands.

Orders are always obeyed, if general and soldiers are in sympathy.

X

GROUND

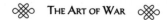

Sun the Master said:

With regard to the different natures of ground there are:

Open ground; broken ground; suspended ground; defiles; precipices; far countries.

Open ground is that where either side has liberty of movement: be quick to occupy any high ground in the neighbourhood and consider well the line of supplies.

Broken ground. Advance is easy, but retreat from it is difficult. Here, if the enemy be not prepared, we may win: but should he be prepared, and defeat us, and retreat be impossible, then there is disaster.

Suspended ground. The side that takes the initiative is under a disadvantage. Here, if the enemy offer some allurement, we should not advance: but rather, by feigning retreat, wait until he has put forth half his force. Then we may attack him with advantage.

Defiles, make haste to occupy; garrison
strongly and await the enemy. Should the
enemy be before you, and in strength, do
not engage him; but if there be unoccupied
points, attack him.

In precipitous ground quickly occupy
a position on a sunny height, and await
the enemy. If the enemy be before you,
withdraw and do not attack him.

If distant from the enemy, and the forces
be equal, to take the initiative is
disadvantageous.

Now, these are the six kinds of ground.
It is the duty of generals to study them.

Again, there are six calamities among the
troops, arising, not from defect of ground, or
lack of opportunity, but from the general's
incapacity.

These are: repulse, relaxation, distress,
disorganisation, confusion and rout.

If troops be sent to attack an enemy of
equal quality, but ten times their number,
they retire discomfited.[1]

Strong soldiers with weak officers cause
relaxation.

Able officers with feeble soldiers cause
distress.

Enraged senior officers, who fall upon the
enemy without orders, and obey not the
general because he does not recognise their
abilities, produce disorganisation.

Weak and amiable generals, whose directions
and leadership are vague, whose
officers' and men's duties are not fixed,
and whose dispositions are contradictory,
produce confusion.

Generals, who are unable to estimate the
enemy, who oppose small numbers to large,
weakness to strength, and who do not put

---

[1] *Utterly defeated.*

picked men in the van of the army, cause
it to be routed.

These six things lead to defeat. It is the
duty of the general to study them carefully.

Ground is the handmaid of victory.

Ability to estimate the enemy, and plan
the victory; an eye for steepness, command
and distances: these are the qualities of the
good general.

Whosoever knows these things, conquers;
he who understands them not, is defeated.

If victory be certain from the military
standpoint, fight, even if the lord forbid.

If defeat be certain from the military
standpoint, do not fight, even though the
lord commands it.

The general who advances, from no
thought of his own glory, retires, regardless
of punishment; but only strives for

the people's welfare, and his lord's advantage,
is a treasure to the state.

The good general cares for his soldiers,
and lovingly treats them as his children;
as a consequence they follow him through
deep valleys, and are beside him in death.

Nevertheless, over-care for the soldiers
may cause disobedience; over-attention may
make them unserviceable; over-indulgence
may produce disorder: they become like
spoilt children, and cannot be used.

He who is confident of his own men, but
is ignorant that the enemy should not be
attacked, has no certainty of victory.

He who knows that the enemy may be
attacked with advantage, but knows not
his own men, has no certainty of victory.

Confidence in the troops, right judgment
when to attack the enemy, but ignorance
of the ground, bring uncertain victory.

The wise soldier, once in motion, does not waver, and is never at a loss.

As has been said: ''Know thyself; know the enemy; fear not for victory.''

Also, if the season and the opportunity be realised, and the ground known, complete victory is certain.

XI

NINE GROUNDS

Sun the Master said:

In respect to the conduct of war there
are:

Distracting ground; disturbing ground;
ground of contention; intersecting ground;
path-ridden ground; deeply-involved ground;
difficult ground; enclosed ground; death
ground.

At all times, when the prince fights in his
own territory, it is called distracting[1] ground.

That ground a short way inside the enemy's
border is called disturbing ground.

Ground giving advantage to whichever
side is in possession, is called ground of
contention.

Ground to which either side has access,
is called intersecting ground.

---

[1] *On distracting ground soldiers are not far from their homes, so a battle
may give them the opportunity to disperse to return to see their families.
An army will be more focused when it fights further away from home
territory.*

Ground between three provinces first
possession of which enables the peoples of
the earth to be controlled, is called path-
ridden ground.

The interior of the enemy's country with
many of his fortified towns in rear, is called
deeply-involved ground.

Mountain and forest, precipices, ravines,
marsh and swamp, all places where passage
is hard, are called difficult ground.

A narrow entrance and winding outlet,
where a small number can oppose a large
force, is called enclosed ground.

That ground where delay means disaster,
is called death ground.

Therefore, do not fight on distracting
ground; do not linger on disturbing ground.

If the enemy be in possession of disputed
ground, do not attack.

In intersecting ground, do not interrupt
the highways.[2]

At the crossing of highways, cultivate
intercourse.[3]

When deeply involved, levy and store
up the enemy's property.

Quickly depart from difficult ground.

On enclosed ground, use stratagem.

On death ground, fight.

The skilful fighters of old were at pains
to disconnect the enemy's front and rear;
they cut asunder small and large forces of
the enemy; prevented mutual help between
his officers and men; spread mistrust
between high and low. They scattered the
enemy, and prevented him from concentrating;
if his soldiers were assembled, they
were without unity.

---

[2] *That the enemy is using.*

[3] *"Cultivate intercourse": join your allies.*

If there be a chance of victory, move; if
there be no chance of success, stand fast.

If I were asked how a powerful and
united force of the enemy should be met,
I would say: lay hands on what the enemy
cherishes and he will conform to our desires.

In war, above all, speed sustains the
spirit of the troops. Strike before the
enemy is ready; and attack his unpreparedness
from an unexpected quarter.

With regard to war in foreign lands.
When strangers in a far country the soldiers
are united and are proof against defeat.
Plunder fertile plains so that the army is
fed; be careful of the health of the soldiers;
do not tire them uselessly; unite their
minds; store up strength; plan well and
secretly. If there be no refuge the soldiers
will not fly from death.

If there be no alternative but death, the
soldiers exert themselves to the utmost.

In desperate places, soldiers lose the sense
of fear.

If there be no place of refuge, there
will be no wavering.

If deeply involved in the enemy's country,
there is unity.

If it be unavoidable, the soldiers will
fight their hardest. Even without warnings
they are vigilant; they comply without
insistence; without stipulations they are
tractable; without explicit instructions they
will trust the general and obey him.

Prohibit the discussion of signs and
omens, and remove the soldiers' doubts;
then to the moment of death they will be
undistracted.

Riches are denied the soldiers, not because
money is a bad thing; old age is forbidden
them, but not because long life is evil.
Hardships and danger are the proper lot
of the soldier.

When the order for attack is given, the
collars of those who are sitting may be wet
with tears; tears may roll down the cheeks

of those reclining; yet these men, in a
desperate place, will fight with the courage
of Chu and Kuei.[4]

Soldiers should be used like the snakes on
Mount Chang; which, if you hit on the head,
the tail will strike you; if you hit the tail,
the head will strike you; if you strike its
middle, head and tail will strike you
together.

---

[4] *Chu, as Lionel Giles explains it, was a native of Wu state and a
contemporary of Sun Tzu's who, in 515 BCE, was asked to kill his
sovereign, Wang Liao. Chu smuggled a knife into a banquet and carried
out the deed, but was immediately set upon by the king's guards and
hacked to pieces. Ts'ao Kuei had been made famous by an act 166 years
earlier, in 681 BCE. Giles' recounting of the story is worth noting in full:
"Lu [the state] had been thrice defeated by Chi, and was just about to
conclude a treaty surrendering a large slice of territory, when Tsao Kuei
suddenly seized Huan Kung, the Duke of Chi, as he stood on the altar
steps and held a dagger against his chest. None of the duke's retainers
dared to move a muscle, and Tsao Kuei proceeded to demand full
restitution, declaring the Lu was being unjustly treated because she was a
smaller and a weaker state. Huan Kung, in peril of his life, was obliged
to consent, whereupon Tsao Kuei flung away his dagger and quietly
resumed his place amid the terrified assemblage without having so much
as changed colour. As was to be expected, the Duke wanted afterwards to
repudiate the bargain, but his wise old counselor Kuan Chung pointed
out to him the impolicy of breaking his word, and the upshot was that this
bold stroke regained for Lu the whole of what she had lost in three pitched
battles."*

Should any one ask me whether men
can be made to move like these snakes,
I say, yes. The men of Wu and Yueh
hate each other; yet, if they cross a river
in the same boat and a storm overtake
them, they help each other like the two
hands.

The horses may be tied, and the chariot
wheels sunk in the mud; but that does not
prevent flight.

Universal courage and unity depend on
good management.

The best results from both the weak and
strong are obtained by a proper use of the
ground.

The skilful warrior can lead his army, as
a man leads another by the hand, because
he places it in a desperate position.

The general should be calm, inscrutable,
just and prudent. He should keep his
officers and men in ignorance of his plans,
and inform no one of any changes or fresh

departures. By changing his camps, and taking devious and unexpected routes, his plans cannot be guessed.

As one taking away the ladder from under those mounted upon the roof, so acts the general when his men are assembled to fight. He penetrates into the heart of the enemy's country and then divulges his plans. He drives the army hither and thither like a flock of sheep, knowing not whither they go.

Therefore the general should assemble the armies, and place them in a desperate position.

The different natures of the Nine Grounds; the suiting of the means to the occasion; the hearts of men: these are things that must be studied.

When deep in the interior of a hostile country, there is cohesion; if only on the borders, there is distraction. To leave home and cross the borders is to be free from interference.

On distracting ground, unite the soldiers'
minds.

On disturbing ground, keep together.

On disputed ground, try to take the
enemy in rear.

On intersecting ground, look well to the
defences.

On path-ridden ground, cultivate intercourse.

On deeply-involved ground be careful
of supplies.

On difficult ground, do not linger.

On enclosed ground, close the path of
escape.

On death ground, show the soldiers that
there is no chance of survival.

It is the nature of soldiers to defend when
surrounded, to fight with energy when

compelled thereto, to pursue the enemy if he retreat.

He cannot treat with other rulers who knows not their ambitions.[5]

He who knows not mountain and forest; cliffs; ravines; lakes and marshes; cannot conduct an army.

He who does not use guides, cannot take advantage of the ground.

He who has not a complete knowledge of the Nine Grounds, cannot gain military dominion.

The great general, when attacking a powerful nation, prevents the enemy from concentrating his hosts.

He overawes the enemy so that other states cannot join against him.

He does not struggle for the favour of other states; nor is he careful of their

---

[5] *As earlier noted, two states that frequently battled each other.*

rights. He has confidence in himself, and awes the enemy.

Therefore he easily takes the fortress, or reduces the country to subjection.

In the bestowal of rewards, or in his orders, he is not bound by ancient rule.

He manages his forces as though they were one man.

Orders should direct the soldiers; but while what is advantageous should be made known, what is disadvantageous should be concealed.

If the forces be plunged into danger, there is survival; from death ground there is retrieval; for the force in danger gains the victory.

Discover the enemy's intentions by conforming to his movements. When these are discovered, then, with one stroke, the general may be killed, even though he be one hundred leagues distant.

When war is declared, close the barriers;
destroy passports; prevent the passage of
the enemy's spies; conduct the business
of the government with vigilance.

Take immediate advantage of the enemy's
weakness; discover what he most values,
and plan to seize it.

Shape your plans according to rule, and
the circumstances of the enemy.

At first behave with the discretion of a
maiden; then, when the enemy gives an
opening, dart in like a rabbit.

The enemy cannot defend himself.

XII

ASSAULT BY FIRE

Sun the Master said:
There are five ways of attack by fire:

The first is called barrack burning; the
second, commissariat burning; the third,
equipment burning; the fourth, store
burning; the fifth, the company burning.

The moment for the fire assault must
be suitable. Further, appliances must
always be kept at hand.

There is a time and day proper for the
setting and carrying out of the fire assault;
namely: such time as the weather is dry;
and a day when the moon is in the quarters
of the stars Chi, Pi, I, Chen[1]: for these
are days of wind.

Regard well the developments that will
certainly arise from the fire, and act upon
them. When fire breaks out inside the
enemy's camp, thrust upon him with all

---

[1] *Lionel Giles' interpretation of this line: "The proper season is when the
weather is very dry; the special days are those days when the moon is in the
constellations of the Sieve, the Wall, the Wing or the Cross-bar."*

speed from without; but if his soldiers be
quiet, wait, and do not attack.

When the fire is at its height, attack or
not as opportunity may arise.

If the opportunity be favourable, set fire
to the enemy's camp, and do not wait for
it to break out from within.

When fire breaks out on the windward
side, do not attack from the leeward.

Wind that rises in the day lasts long.
Wind that rises in the night time quickly
passes away.

The peculiarities of the five burnings
must be known, and the calendar studied,
and, if the attack is to be assisted, the fire
must be unquenchable.

If water is to assist the attack, the flood
must be overwhelming.

Water may isolate or divide the enemy;
fire may consume his camp; but unless

victory or possession be obtained, the enemy
quickly recovers, and misfortunes arise. The
war drags on, and money is spent.

Let the enlightened lord consider well;
and the good general keep the main object
in view. If no advantage is to be gained
thereby, do not move; without prospect of,
victory, do not use the soldiers; do not
fight unless the state be in danger.

War should not be undertaken because
the lord is in a moment of passion. The
general must not fight because there is
anger in his heart.

Do not make war unless victory may be
gained thereby; if there be prospect of
victory, move; if there be no prospect,
do not move.

For passion may change to gladness,
anger passes away; but a country, once
overturned, cannot be restored; the dead
cannot be brought to life.

Therefore it is written, the enlightened lord is circumspect, and the good general takes heed; then is the state secure, and the army victorious in battle.

XIII

THE EMPLOYMENT
OF SPIES

Sun the Master said:

Calling 100,000 men to arms, and
transporting them a hundred leagues is such
an undertaking that in one day 1,000 taels[1]
of the citizens' and nobles' money are spent;
commotions arise within and without the
state; carriers fall down exhausted on the
line of march of the army; and the occupations
of 700,000[2] homes are upset.

Again, for years the armies may face each
other; yet the issue may depend on a
single day's victory.

Therefore, by grudging slight expense
in titles and salaries to spies, to remain in
ignorance of the enemy's circumstances, is
to be without humanity. Such a person
is no general; he is no assistance to his

---

[1] *A tael was equivalent to approximately 40 grams, or 1.4 ounces of silver.*

[2] The population was divided for military purposes into groups of eight families. In time of war, each group sent one man into the field, furnished his wants, and provided for his family. Therefore if 100,000 men are taken, 700,000 homes are affected.

lord; he is no master of victory.[3]
The enlightened ruler and the wise
general who act, win, and are distinguished
beyond the common, are informed beforehand.

This knowledge is not to be got by calling
on gods and demons; nor does it come
of past experience nor calculation. It is
through men that knowledge of the enemy
is gained.

Now the five kinds of spies are these:
village spies, inner spies, converted spies,
death spies, living spies.

If these five means be employed
simultaneously, none can discover their working.
This is called the Mysterious Thread: it is
the Lord's Treasure.

Village spies are such people of the
country as give information.

---

[3] *In Sun Tzu's time spies could become national heroes and were seen as
at least important as warriors in securing victories. Sun Tzu's point is
that to save money on not employing spies is a false economy, since the
information they may give could bring an end to a war which might
otherwise have gone on for years, cost countless lives, shattered livelihoods
and drained the state's wealth.*

Inner spies are those of the enemy's
officials employed by us.

Converted spies are those of the enemy's
spies in our pay.

Death[4] spies are sent to misinform the
enemy, and to spread false reports through
our spies already in the enemy's lines.

Living[5] spies return to report.

In connection with the armies, spies
should be treated with the greatest kindness;
and in dealing out reward, they
should receive the most generous treatment.
All matters relating to spies are secret.

Without infinite capacity in the general,
the employment of spies is impossible.
Their treatment requires benevolence and
uprightness. Except they be observed with

---

[4] So called because they are put to death when the enemy finds
out that he has been tricked.
[5] Messengers and others who do not disguise their identity are
included under this heading.

the closest attention, the truth will not be obtained from them.

Wonderful indeed is the power of spies.

There is no occasion when they cannot be used.

If a secret matter be spoken of before the time is ripe, the spy who told the matter, and the man who repeated the same, should be put to death.

If desirous of attacking an army; of besieging a fortress; or of killing a certain person; first of all, learn the names of the general in charge; of his right-hand men; of those who introduce visitors to the Presence; of the gate keeper and the sentries. Then set the spies to watch them.

Seek out the enemy's spies who come to spy on us; give them money; cause them to be lodged and cared for; and convert them to the service. Through them we are enabled to obtain spies among the enemy's villagers and officials.

By means of the converted spy, we can construct a false story for the death spy to carry to the enemy.

It is through the converted spy that we are able to use the five varieties, to their utmost advantage; therefore he must be liberally treated.

In ancient times the rise to power of the province of Yin was due to Ichih, who was sent to the country of Hsia.

Likewise during the foundation of the state of Chu, Luya lived among the people of Shang.[6]

Therefore, intelligent rulers and wise generals use the cleverest men as spies, and invariably acquire great merit. The spy is a necessity to the army. Upon him the movement of the army depends.

---

[6] *Ichih and Luya, illustrious names in the annals of Chinese warfare, are mentioned by Sun Tzu to illustrate that, for it to have a decisive role in state victories, espionage requires the very best people.*

PART II

PART II

THE SAYINGS
OF WUTZU

AN INTRODUCTION
BY TOM BUTLER-BOWDON

The Sayings of Wutzu is translator EF Calthrop's name for the ancient Chinese book of military strategy known as the *Wuzi*. Calthrop wanted to publish the *Sayings* alongside *The Art of War* because he and Sun Tzu were legendary warriors in the same era, and both served the same king. Additionally, as is stated in *The Art of War*, it was Wu Tzu who recommended Sun Tzu to his patron, the King of Wu.

Wutzu, Wu Tzu-hsu, Wu Yuan, or Wu Qui, as he is variously known, was born in the state of Wei. He became its top general, carrying the state to great victories, and as its First Minister helped it to achieve prosperity. As the book notes: "And the kingdom grew and stretched 1,000 leagues on every side, which was all due to the virtue of Wu." He was later employed by the state of Chu, which he also helped to greater power. However, he was something of a reformer and was murdered by a group of nobles who felt threatened by his changes.

In the *Sayings*, Wu Tzu's wisdom is presented in the form of a dialogue between Lord Wen, ruler of the state of Wu (or Wei), and Wu Tzu. We do not know whether Wu penned his *Sayings* himself or whether they were recorded by someone else, but readers will note many similarities in philosophy and detail between the work and *The Art of War*. These include an emphasis on battle strategy; creating unity in the forces; "ground" or the physical factors of waging war; the integrity of the general; and wise management of subordinates and understanding of human motivation.

An interesting aspect of the *Sayings* is its mention of various rulers from history and in the warring states period, including Prince Chengsang, Prince Yuhu, Lord Tang of Cheng, Prince Huan of Chi, Prince Mu of Chin, and Lord Chuang of Chu. Their stories are used to illustrate good or bad points of military strategy and preparedness.

Below are some of Wu Tzu's main lessons, along with comments on their potential usefulness to us today.

RIGHT ACTION

Echoing Sun Tzu's admonition to avoid actual fighting wherever possible, Wu Tzu lists the reasons why a state goes to war. The only *just* one, he notes, is "the prevention of tyranny and the restoration of order." In general, he emphasizes "propriety," or accordance with the conventional rules of good behavior, as the basis for action:

wise men maintain order by keeping in the Way, and governing with righteousness; they move with discretion, and with benevolence they make the people amenable.

This is the "Way" that Sun Tzu discusses. For Wu Tzu, propriety is the glue that holds together any state, society, or army. With standards for moral action in place, people live up to them and you have order. When these standards are not followed, chaos reigns.

The lesson of Wu Tzu's propriety in a modern context is that the organization you manage must *stand for something* (think of Google's maxim, "Don't be evil"), and it must have accepted, clear norms of behavior that all are expected to follow. At an individual level, propriety means acting in accord with your conscience, or being true to your own previously set code of behavior and action.

DOMINATE

In Chapter I, "The Government of a Country," Wu Tzu notes:

For those who have gained power on earth by many victories are few; and those who have lost it, many.

It is better to have one complete, major victory, he says, than a succession of smaller ones that wear out a people and a state. If you do have to go to war, prepare long and hard for it and put everything into achieving a decisive rout. The aim in war is to achieve *dominion*.

The message we can take from this: It is a waste of your time and resources to merely aim to "do well" in your career. Your purpose must be to dominate your field – and you can, as long as you are prepared to do the work and act sagely.

MOTIVATE

Strongly echoing *The Art of War*, Wu Tzu emphasizes unity in the ranks as the basis of achieving victory:

> *Therefore, wise rulers who would employ their subjects in great endeavours, should first establish harmony among them.*

Wu Tzu explains how the wise general organizes soldiers into companies or groups. This is not done randomly or automatically, but requires keen observation of individual soldiers. For instance, one should put people together who have a similar capability or level of skill, which creates a strong team. More interestingly, he observes, one should group together all those who have experienced a loss of face of some kind, as their desire to redeem themselves will make for a powerful unit.

It seems obvious to put the right people in the right places, but Wu Tzu notes that if you do so, victory is almost assured. In terms of the upper echelons of the army, he observes that "good advisers are the foundation of an empire."

Wu Tzu is a master of human nature, understanding the power of punishment and reward to build a great army. He urges for a system that is just, in which people know exactly what befalls them if they desert the field or steal from the stores, but equally the prizes that await them if they succeed. Wu Tzu places much importance on rewarding the best performers, including giving gifts to their wives and children. He notes:

In every army there are mighty warriors . . . swifter of foot than the war horse; who can take the enemy's standard, or slay his general. If such men be selected, and set apart, cared for and honoured, they are the life of the army.

He goes on to say:

> *If these men be well selected, double their number can be defeated.*

At this, you may recall Microsoft co-founder Bill Gates' well-known remark that, without a super-talented core of just 20 people, his company (which employs thousands of people) would never have got going. Though it was a tough and unforgiving place to work (if you did not live and breathe Microsoft, you were replaced), Gates also instituted a very clear system of reward that created thousands of millionaires and more than a few billionaires. The "us against them" mentality that has defined the company and created a fiery sense of mission is straight out of Wu Tzu and Sun Tzu.

ATTACK

With the anxiety of any threatened ruler, Lord Wen says to Wu Tzu:

> *Chin threatens us on the west; Chu surrounds us on the south; Chao presses us in the north; Chi watches us in the east; Yen stops our rear, and Han is posted in our front. Thus, the armies*

of six nations encompass us on every side, and our condition is very unpropitious. Canst thou relieve my anxiety?

Wu Tzu calms him down by noting that vigilance is the key, and that they still have time to gather intelligence and organize the state's forces.

Indeed, large sections of the *Sayings*, particularly Chapters II and V, "Estimation of the enemy" and "Suiting the occasion," are preoccupied with knowledge of the enemy and knowledge of the terrain. If anything, Wu Tzu is more insistent on these points than Sun Tzu, underscoring that different opponents must be engaged with different tactics, depending on their strengths and weaknesses. The crucial point to remember is that the enemy must only be attacked when it is in a vulnerable position or state. In doing so, one can achieve a decisive victory with the minimum use of resources.

Today's businessperson would do well to absorb these sections, not for the details but to really grasp the idea that one should only engage a competitor having first discovered their weakness, or that in launching a new product or service you must exhaustively study market conditions and the intended audience.

FINAL WORD

Wu Tzu's *Sayings* provide an excellent complement to *The Art of War*, reminding us to follow the "Way" of right and powerful action. This way is based on planning and preparedness, respect for order, self-knowledge, knowledge of the opponent, and awareness of the right time to make a move.

Though Wu Tzu was perhaps a rougher character than Sun Tzu and had a ruthless reputation, his understanding of power and strategy was second to none. In your work and life, it would be difficult to go wrong following his guidance; in fact, doing so may be the source of your greatest success.

Tom Butler-Bowdon, 2010

CONTENTS

INTRODUCTION

Now Wu, albeit clothed in the raiment
of a scholar, was a man skilled in the
art of war.

And Wen, Lord of Wei, came unto
him and said:

"I am a man of peace, caring not for
military affairs."

And Wu said:

"Your actions are witnesses of your
mind; why do your words say not what is
in your heart?

"You do prepare and dress hides and
leather through the four seasons, ornamenting
them with red lacquer and the figures
of panthers and elephants; which give not
warmth in winter, neither in summer,

coolness. Moreover, you make halberds,[1] 24[2] feet long, and pikes 12 feet long, and leather (covered) chariots so large as to fill up the gateways, wheels with ornament, and naves capped with leather. Now, these are neither beautiful to the eye nor light in the chase; I know not for what use my lord makes these things.

"But, although provided with these instruments of war, if the leader be not competent, a brooding hen might as well strike a badger, or a dog with young challenge the tiger: the spirit of encounter may be present, but there is no end but death.

"In ancient times, the Prince Chengsang cultivated virtue, and put away military things, and his kingdom fell.

"The Prince Yuhu put his trust in numbers, and delighted in war and was driven from the throne.

---

[1] *Weapon with a long shaft and axe-like blade.*
[2] All numbers connected with weapons were Yin, that is to say even, or belonging to the negative principle of Chinese philosophy from their connection with death.

"Therefore the enlightened ruler should
ponder over these things; encourage learning
and virtue in the kingdom, and be prepared
against war from without.

"To hesitate before the enemy is not a
cause for righteousness; remorse for the
fallen is not true humanity."

And when Lord Wen heard these words,
he himself spread a seat, and his wife
offered up a cup, and Wu was appointed
general before the altar.

Now, in the defence of Hsihe against
different states there were fought seventy-six
great fights, of which sixty-four were
complete victories, and the remainder un-
decided.

And the kingdom grew and stretched 1,000
leagues on every side, which was all due
to the virtue of Wu.

1

THE GOVERNMENT
OF A COUNTRY

And Wu the Master said:

The mighty rulers of old first trained
their retainers, and then extended their
regard to their outlying feudatories.[1]

There are four discords:

Discord in the state: then never make war.

Discord in the army: then do not strike
camp.

Discord in the camp: then do not advance
to attack.

Discord in the battle array: then seek
not to decide the issue.

Therefore, wise rulers who would employ
their subjects in great endeavours, should
first establish harmony among them.

Lend not a ready ear to human counsellors,
but lay the matter before the altar; seek

---

[1] Estates held by feudal tenure or right.

inside the turtle,[2] and consider well the time and season. Then, if all be well, commit ourselves to the undertaking.

If the people know that their lord is careful of their lives, and laments their death beyond all else; then, in the time of danger, the soldiers advance, and, advancing, find glory in death; and in survival after retreat, dishonour.

The Master said:

The Way must follow the only true path: righteousness lies at the root of achievement and merit.

The object of stratagem is to avoid loss and gain advantage.

The object of government is to guard enterprise and to preserve the state.

---

[2] The back of a turtle was burnt and the answer was ascertained by the manner in which the shell split. Wu Tzu advises the seeking of spiritual guidance for actions, using a particular kind of oracle.

If conduct depart from the Way, and
the undertaking accord not with
righteousness, then disaster befalls the mighty.

Therefore, wise men maintain order by
keeping in the Way, and governing with
righteousness; they move with discretion,
and with benevolence they make the people
amenable.

If these four virtues be practised, there
is prosperity; if they be neglected, there
is decay.

For, when Lord Tang of Cheng defeated
Lord Chieh, the people of Hsia rejoiced,
and when Wu of Chou defeated Lord
Chou, the people of Yin were not
discomfited. And this was because it was
ordained by Providence and human desire.

The Master said:

In the government of a country and
command of an army, the inculcation of
propriety, stimulation of righteousness, and
the promotion of a sense of shame are
required.

When men possess a sense of shame,
they will attack with resolution when in
strength, and when few in number defend
to the last.

But while victory is easy in attack, it
is difficult in defence.

Now, of the fighting races below heaven;
those who gained five victories have been
worn out; those who have won four victories
have been impoverished; three victories
have given dominion; two victories have
founded a kingdom; and upon one victory
an empire has been established.

For those who have gained power on
earth by many victories are few; and those
who have lost it, many.

The Master said:
The causes of war are five:

First, ambition; second, profit; third,
overburdened hate; fourth, internal
disorder; fifth, famine.

Again, the natures of war are five:

First, a righteous war; second, a war of might; third, a war of revenge; fourth, a war of tyranny; fifth, an unrighteous war.

The prevention of tyranny and the restoration of order is just; to strike in reliance on numbers is oppression; to raise the standard for reasons of anger is a war of revenge; to quit propriety,[3] and seize advantage is tyranny; when the state is disordered and the people worn out, to harbour designs, and set a multitude in motion, is a war of unrighteousness.

There is a way of overcoming each of these five.

Righteousness is overcome by propriety; might by humanity; revenge by words; tyranny by deception; unrighteousness by strategy.

_____

[3] Conformity to conventional standards of good or proper behaviour.

Lord Wen asked and said:

"I would know the way to control an
army, to measure men, and make the
country strong."

Wu answered and said:

"The enlightened rulers of antiquity
respected propriety between sovereign and
people; established etiquette between high
and low; settled officials and citizens in close
accord; gave instruction in accordance with
custom; selected men of ability, and thereby
provided against what should come to pass.

"In ancient times, Prince Huan of Chi
assembled 50,000 men at arms, and became
chief among the princes; Prince Wen of
Chin put 40,000 mighty men in the van,[4]
and gained his ambition; Prince Mu of
Chin gathered together 80,000 invincibles,
and subdued his neighbouring foes.
Therefore, the princes of powerful states must
consider their people, and assemble the

---

[4] Vanguard, or front of an advancing army.

valiant and spirited men by companies.

"Those who delight to attack, and to display their valour and fealty should be formed in companies.

"Those skilful in scaling heights, or covering long distances, and who are quick and light of foot must be collected in companies.

"Retainers who have lost their rank, and who are desirous of displaying their prowess before their superiors should be gathered into companies.

"Those who have abandoned a castle, or deserted their trust, and are desirous of atoning for their misconduct, should be collected and formed into companies.

"These five bodies form the flower of the army. With 8,000 of such troops, if they issue from within, an encompassing enemy can be burst asunder; if they enter from without, a castle can be overthrown."

Lord Wen asked and said:

"I desire to know how to fix the battle
array, render defence secure, and attack
with certainty of victory."

Wu answered and said:

"To see with the eye is better than ready
words. Yet, I say, if the wise men be put
in authority and the ignorant in low places,
then the army is already arranged.

"If the people be free from anxiety
about their estates, and love their officials,
then defence is already secure.

"If all the lieges be proud of their lord,
and think ill of neighbouring states, then
is the battle already won."

The Lord Wen once assembled a number
of his subjects to discuss affairs of state:
and none could equal him in wisdom, and
when he left the council chamber his face
was pleased.

Then Wu advanced and said:

"In ancient times, Lord Chuang of Chu
once consulted with his lieges, and none were
like unto him in wisdom; and when the
Lord left the council chamber his
countenance was troubled. Then the Duke Shen
asked and said: 'Why is my Lord
troubled?' And he answered: 'I have
heard that the world is never without sages,
and that in every country there are wise
men; that good advisers are the foundation
of an empire; and friends of dominion.
Now, if I, lacking wisdom, have no equal
among the multitude of my officers,
dangerous indeed is the state of Chu. It grieves
me that whereas Prince Chuang of Chu
was troubled in a like case my Lord should
be pleased.'"

And hearing this Lord Wen was inwardly
troubled.

11

ESTIMATION OF
THE ENEMY

And Lord Wen said to Wu:

"Chin threatens us on the west; Chu surrounds us on the south; Chao presses us in the north; Chi watches us in the east; Yen stops our rear; and Han is posted in our front. Thus, the armies of six nations encompass us on every side, and our condition is very unpropitious. Canst thou relieve my anxiety?"

Wu answered and said:

"The path of safety of a state lies first of all in vigilance. Now my Lord has already taken warning, therefore misfortunes are yet distant.

"Let me state the habits of these six countries. The forces of Chi are weighty but without solidity; the soldiers of Chin are scattered, and fight each of his own accord: the army of Chu is well ordered, but cannot endure: the soldiers of Yen defend well, but are without dash: the armies of the three Chins are well governed, but cannot be used.

"The nature of Chi is stubborn and the country rich, but prince and officials are proud and luxurious, and neglectful of the common people; government is loose and rewards not impartial; in one camp there are two minds; the front is heavy, but the rear is light. Therefore it is ponderous without stability. To attack it, the force must be divided into three parts, and, by threatening it on three sides, its front can be broken.

"The nature of Chin is strong, the country rugged, and the government firm; rewards and punishments just, the people indomitable, and all have the fighting spirit; therefore, when separated, each fights of his own accord.

"To defeat this people, they must first be tempted by gain to leave their cause, so that the soldiers, greedy of profit, desert their general: then, taking advantage of their disobedience, their scattered forces can be erased, ambushes laid, favourable opportunities taken, and their general captured.

"The nature of Chu is weak, its territory
wide, the government weak, and the people
exhausted; the troops are well ordered but
of short endurance.

"The way to defeat them is to assault
their camp, throw it into concision[1] and
crush their spirit, advance softly, and retire
quickly; tire them out, avoid a serious
encounter, and they may be defeated.

"The nature of Yen is straightforward;
its people are cautious, loving courage and
righteousness, and without guile; wherefore
they defend but are not daring.

"The way to defeat them is to draw
close and press them; tease them and pass
to a distance; move quickly, and appear in
the rear, thus causing bewilderment to their
officers amid fear in their ranks. Our chariots
and horsemen will act with circumspection
and avoid encounter. Thus their general
can be captured.

---

[1] Meaning cut up into pieces.

"The three Chins are the middle kingdom:
their nature is peaceful and their
rule just. Their people are tired of war;
their troops are trained, but their leaders
are despised; pay is small, and the soldiers
lack the spirit of sacrifice, thus they are well
governed but cannot be used.

"The way to defeat them is to threaten
them from afar. If a multitude attack –
defend; if they retreat – pursue, and tire
them out.

"In every army there are mighty warriors
with strength to lift the Censer,[2] swifter
of foot than the war horse, who can take
the enemy's standard, or slay his general.
If such men be selected, and set apart,
cared for and honoured, they are the life
of the army.

"Those who use the five arms[3] with skill,
who are clever, strong and quick, and

---

[2] Large container of incense, burned during religious
ceremonies.
[3] Halberd, shield, javelin, pike, and short pike.

careless of the enemy, should be given rank
and decoration, and used to decide the
victory. Their parents and families should
be cared for, encouraged by rewards, and
kept in fear of punishment. These men
consolidate the battle array; their presence
causes endurance.

"If these men be well selected, double
their number can be defeated."

And Lord Wen said:

"It is good!"

Wu the Master said:

"In the estimation of the enemy there
are eight cases when, without consulting
the oracles,[4] he may be attacked.

"First, an enemy who, in great wind and
cold, has risen early, started forth across ice

---

[4] Meaning, what to do in these situations is so obvious no
oracular guidance is required.

and rivers, and braved stress and hardships.

"Second, an enemy who, in the height of
summer, and in great heat, has risen early, has
travelled incessantly, is hungry and without
water, and is striving to reach a distance.

"Third, an enemy who has been encamped long
in one place, who is without
provisions, when the fanners are vexed
and indignant, who has suffered frequent
calamities, and whose officers are unable
to establish confidence.

"Fourth, when the enemy's funds are
exhausted, fuel and fodder scarce; when
the heavens have been overcast by long
continued rain; when there is the desire to
loot, but no place to loot withal.

"Fifth, when their numbers are few;
when water is scarce; when men and horses
are scourged by pestilence, and from no
quarter is succour at hand.

"Sixth, when night falls, and the way is
yet far; when officers and men are worn

out and fearful, weary and without food, and have laid aside their armour and are resting.

"Seventh, when the general's authority is weak, the officials false, and the soldiers unsettled; when their army has been alarmed, and no help is forthcoming.

"Eighth, when the battle formation is not yet fixed, or camp pitched; when climbing a hill, or passing through a difficult place; when half is hidden and half exposed.

"An enemy in these situations may be smitten without hesitation.

"There are six enemies, that, without consulting oracles, should be avoided.

"First, wide and vast territories, and a large and rich population.

"Second, where the officials care for the people, and bestow bountiful favours and rewards.

"Third, where rewards are well deserved, punishment accurately apportioned, and

operations undertaken only when the time
is fitting.

"Fourth, where merit is recognised and
given rank, wise men appointed, and ability
employed.

"Fifth, where the troops are many and
their weapons excellent.

"Sixth, when help is at hand on every
side, or from a powerful ally.

"For, if the enemy excel in the foregoing,
he must be avoided without hesitation. As
it is written, if it be judged good, advance;
if it be known to be difficult, retreat."

And Lord Wen asked and said:

"I desire to know how the interior of
the enemy can be known from his outer
appearance; the form of his camp by
observing his advance, and how victory
may be determined?"

And Wu answered and said:

"If the coming of the enemy be reckless
like roaring waters, his banners and pennons[5]
disordered, and horses and men frequently
looking behind, then ten can be struck with
one. Panic will certainly seize them.

"Before the various princes have
assembled, before harmony has been
established between lord and lieges, before
ditches have been dug, or regulations
established, and the army is alarmed;
wishing to advance, but unable; wishing
to retreat, but unable: then the force can
strike twice their numbers, and in a
hundred fights there is no fear of retreat."

Lord Wen asked:

"How can the enemy be certainly
defeated?"

---

[5] Flag or pennant. In ancient Chinese warfare, banners, flags,
gongs and drums were employed as means of communication
within an army.

Chi answered and said:

"Make certain of the enemy's real condition and quickly strike his weak point; strike an enemy who has just arrived from afar, before his ranks are arranged; or one who has eaten and has not completed his dispositions; or an enemy who is hurrying about, or is busily occupied; or has not made favourable use of the ground, or has let pass the opportunity; or one who has come a long distance, and those in rear are late and have not rested.

"Strike an enemy who is half across waters; or who is on a difficult or narrow road; or whose flags and banners are in confusion; or who is frequently changing position; or whose general is not in accord with the soldiers; or who is fearful.

"All such should be assaulted by the picked men; and the remainder of the army should be divided, and follow after them. They may be attacked at once without hesitation."

III

CONTROL OF THE ARMY

Lord Wen said:

"What is of first importance in operations of war?"

Wu answered and said:

"Lightness, of which there are four natures, Weight, of which there are two natures, and Confidence must be clearly comprehended."

And Wen said:

"What are these?"

And Wu answered:

"If the way be easy, the horses are light of foot; if the horses be light of foot, the chariots travel freely; if the chariots travel easily, men can ride in them without difficulty; if the men be free to move, the fight prospers. If the difficult and easy ways be known, the horses are lightened; if the horses be fed at proper intervals, the chariots are swift; if there be plenty of oil

on the axles of the chariots, the riders are
quickly conveyed; if the spears be sharp
and the armour strong, the men make the
fight easy.

"Large rewards in advance, heavy
punishment in retreat, and impartiality
in their bestowal are required.

"He who well understands these things
is the master of victory."

And Lord Wen asked and said:

"By what means can the army gain the
victory?"

And Wu answered:

"The foundation of victory is good
government."

Again, Wen asked and said:

"Is it not determined by numbers?"

And Wu replied:

"If laws and orders be not clear; if
rewards and punishments be not just; if
the bell be sounded and they halt not, or
drum be beaten and men do not advance;
even if there be a hundred thousand men
at arms, they are of no avail.

"Where there is order, then there is
propriety at rest, and dignity in motion;
none can withstand the attack, and retreat
forbids pursuit; motion is regulated, and
movements to right and left are made in
answer to the signal; if the ranks be
cut asunder, formation is preserved; if
scattered, they are maintained; in fortune
or in danger, there is unity; if a number
be collected, they cannot be separated;
they may be used but not wearied; in
whatever situation they are placed, nothing
under heaven can withstand them. The
army may be called a father and his
children."

And Wu said:

"In marching, movements and halts must
be properly adjusted, suitable occasions for

rationing not missed; the strength of men
and horses not exhausted. If these three
things be observed, the commands of the
superior can be carried out; if the commands
of the superior be carried out, order is
maintained. If advances and halts be without
method, victualling unsuitable, horses and
men tired and weary – neither unsaddled or
housed – it is because the orders cannot
be obeyed; if the orders be set aside,
there is disorder in the camp, and in
battle – defeat.''

Wu the Master said:

''On that depository of corpses, the
battlefield, if there be certain expectation of
death, there is life; if there be happy
expectation of life, there is death. The
good general is like unto one sitting in
a leaking ship, or lying under a burning
roof; the wisest man cannot contrive
against him; the strongest man cannot
destroy his composure; and the enemy's
onslaught can be withstood. For
procrastination is the greatest enemy of the
general; disasters to the army are born of

indecision.''

Wu the Master said:

''Men meet their death from lack of
ability or unskilfulness. Therefore training
is the first requirement of war. One man
with a knowledge of war can teach ten; ten
men skilled in war can teach one hundred;
one hundred can teach one thousand; one
thousand can teach ten thousand; and ten
thousand men can train an army.

''An enemy from a distance should be
awaited, and struck at short range; an
enemy that is tired should be met in good
order; hunger should be opposed by full
bellies; the battle formation should be
round or square, the men should kneel or
stand; go or remain; move to the right
or left; advance or retire; concentrate or
disperse; close or extend when the signal
is given.

''All these changes must be learnt, and
the weapons distributed. This is the
business of the general.''

Wu the Master said:

"In the teaching of war, spears are given
to the short; bows and catapults to the tall;
banners and standards to the strong; the
bell and drum to the bold; fodder and
provisions to the feeble; the arrangement
of the plan to the wise. Men of the same
district should be united; and groups and
squads should help each other. At one
beat of the drum the ranks are put in
order; at two beats of the drum, formation
will be made; at three beats of the drum,
food will be issued; at four beats of the
drum, the men will prepare to march; at
five beats of the drum, ranks will be formed;
when the drums beat together, then the
standards will be raised."

And Lord Wen asked and said:

"What is the way of marching and halting
an army?"

And Wu answered:

"Natural ovens and dragons' heads should
be avoided. Natural ovens are the mouths

of large valleys. Dragons' heads are the extremities of large mountains. The green dragons (banners) should be placed on the left, and the white tigers on the right; the red sparrows in front; the snakes and tortoises behind; the pole star (standard) above; and the soldiers will look to the standard.

"When going forth to battle, the direction of the wind must be studied; if blowing in the direction of the enemy, the soldiers will be assembled and follow the wind; if a head wind, the position will be strengthened, and a wait made for the wind to change."

And Lord Wen asked and said:

"In what way should horses be treated?"

And Wu answered and said:

"The places where they are kept should be made comfortable; fodder should be suitable and timely. In winter their stables should be warmed, and in summer sheltered from the heat; their coats clipped, their

feet carefully pared, their attention directed
so that they be not alarmed, their paces
regulated, and their going and halting
trained; horses and men should be in accord,
and then the horses can be used. The
harness, the saddle, bit, bridle, and reins
must be strong; if the horse be without
vice at the beginning, he can be used to
the end; if the horse be hungry it is good;
if his belly be full, his value decreases; if
the sun be falling and the way still long,
dismount frequently. For it is proper that
the men be worked, but the horses must be
used with discretion, so that they may be
prepared should the enemy suddenly attack
us.

"If these things be well known, then
there is free passage under heaven."

IV

QUALITIES OF THE
GENERAL

Wu the Master said:

"The leader of the army is one who is master of both arms and letters. He who is both brave and tender can be entrusted with troops.

"In the popular estimation of generals, courage alone is regarded; nevertheless, courage is but one of the qualifications of the leader. Courage is heedless in encounter; and rash encounter, which is ignorant of the consequences, cannot be called good.

"There are five matters which leaders must carefully consider.

"First, reason; second, preparation; third, determination; fourth, vigilance; fifth, simplicity.

"With reason, a multitude can be controlled like a small number.

"Preparedness sees an enemy outside the gate.

"Determination before the enemy has no thought of life.

"Even after a victory, vigilance behaves as before the first encounter.

"Simplicity ensures few regulations, and preserves order.

"When the leader receives his orders, he forthwith departs. Not until the enemy has been vanquished does he speak of return. This is the duty of the general.

"Wherefore, from the day of departure of the army, the general seeks glory in death, and dreams not of return in dishonour."

Wu the Master said:

"In war there are four important influences.

"First, spirit; second, ground; third, opportunity; fourth, force.

"The military value of the nation's forces – of one hundred times ten thousand fighting men – depends upon the personality of one man alone; this is called the influence of spirit.

"When the road is steep and narrow, when there are famous mountains and fastnesses where ten men can defend and one thousand cannot pass them by; such is the influence of ground.

"When spies have been skilfully sown, and mounted men pass to and from the enemy's camp, so that his masses are divided, his sovereign and ministers vexed with each other, and superiors and inferiors mutually censorious; this is the moment of opportunity.

"When the linch-pins are secure, the oars and sweeps ready for use in the boats, the armed men trained for war, and the horses exercised, we have what is called the influence of force.

"He who understands these four matters has the qualifications of a general.

Furthermore, dignity, virtue, benevolence,
courage, are needed to lead the troops, to calm
the multitude, to put fear in the enemy,
to remove doubts. When orders are
issued, the subordinates do not defy them.
Wheresoever the army is, that place the
enemy avoids. If these four virtues be
present, the country is strong; if they be
not present, the country is overthrown.

"Of such is the good general."

Wu the Master said:

"The use of drums and bells is to attract
the ear; of flags, standards, and banners to
strike the eye; of laws and penalties to
put fear in the heart.

"To attract the ear the sound must be
clear; to strike the eye the colours must
be bright. The heart is awed by punishment,
therefore punishment must be strict.

"If these three matters be not ordered,
the state may, by chance, be preserved,
but defeat by the enemy is certain.

Therefore, as it has been said (if these three things be present), there is no departing from the commands of the general; when he orders, there is no going back from death.''

Wu the Master said:

''The secret of war is, first, to know who is the enemy's general, and to judge his ability. If our plans depend on his dispositions, then success will be achieved without toil.

''If their general be stupid, and heedlessly trustful, he may be enticed by fraud; if he be avaricious and careless of his fame, he may be bribed with gifts. If he make unconsidered movements without plan, he should be tired out and placed in difficulties. If the superiors be wealthy and proud, and the inferiors avaricious and resentful, they should be set against each other. An enemy that is undetermined, now advancing and then retreating, whose soldiers have nought wherein to put their trust, should be alarmed, and put to flight.

"When an enemy thinks lightly of the general, and desires to return home, the easy roads should be blocked, and the difficult and narrow roads opened; await their coming and capture them.

"If their advance be easy and retreat difficult, await their coming and then advance against them.

"If their advance be difficult and retreat easy, then press and strike them.

"An army that is camped in marshy ground, where there are no water-courses, and long and frequent rains, should be inundated.

"An army that is camped in wild marshes, covered with dark and overhanging grass and brambles, and swept by frequent high winds, should be overthrown by fire.

"An army that has halted long without moving; whose general and soldiers have grown careless, and neglect precautions,

should be approached by stealth, and taken
by surprise.''

Lord Wen asked, saying:

''If the two armies be facing each other,
and the name of the enemy's general
unknown, in what manner can we discover
it?''

And Wu answered and said:

''A brave man of low degree, lightly
but well equipped, should be employed.
He should think only of flight and naught
of advantage. Then, if he observe the
enemy's pursuit, if there be first a halt
and then an advance, order is established.
If we retreat and the enemy pursue, but
pretend not to be able to overtake us,
see an advantage but pretend not to be
aware of it, then their general may be
called a wise general, and conflict with
him must be avoided. If their army be
full of uproar; their banners and standards
disordered, their soldiers going about or
remaining of their own accord, some in

line, others in column; if such an enemy
be eager to pursue, and see an advantage
which they are desperate to seize, then
their general is a fool: even if there be
a host, they may be taken.''

V

SUITING THE OCCASION

Lord Wen asked and said:

"If strong chariots, good horses, strong and valiant soldiers suddenly meet the enemy, and are thrown into confusion, and ranks broken, what should be done?"

And Wu answered and said:

"In general, the method of fighting is to effect order in daylight by means of flags and banners, pennons and batons; at night by gongs and drums, whistles and flutes. If a signal be made to the left, the troops move to the left; if to the right, they move to the right. Advance is made at the sound of the drum; halt at the sound of the gong; one blast of the whistle is for advance, two for the rally. If those who disobey be cut down, the forces are subject to authority. If officers and soldiers carry out orders, a superior enemy cannot exist; no position is impregnable in the attack."

Lord Wen asked and said:

"What is to be done if the enemy be
many and we be few?"

And Wu answered and said:

"Avoid such an enemy on open ground,
and meet him in the narrow way; for,
as it is written, if 1 is to stand against
1,000, there is naught better than a pass;
if 10 are to hold against 100, there is
nothing better than a steep place; if
1,000 are to strike 10,000, there is nothing
better than a difficult place. If a small
force, with beat of gong and drum, suddenly
arise in a narrow way, even a host will
be upset. Therefore it is written: "He
who has a multitude seeks the plain, and
he who has few seeks the narrow way."

And Lord Wu asked and said:

"A mighty host,[1] strong and courageous,
which is on the defence with a mountain
behind, a precipice between, high ground

---

[1] Army.

on the right, and a river on the left, with
deep moats, and high walls, and which has
artillery; whose retreat is like the removal
of a mountain, advance like the hurricane,
and whose supplies are in abundance, is
an enemy against whom long defence is
difficult. In effect, what should be done
in such a case?''

And Wu answered and said:

''This indeed is a great question, whose
issue depends, not upon the might of
chariot and horse, but upon the schemes
of a wise man.

''Let 1,000 chariots and 10,000 horse, well
equipped and with foot-men added to them,
be divided into five armies, and a road
allotted to each army.

''Then if there be five armies, and each
army take a different road, the enemy will
be puzzled, and know not in what quarter
to be prepared. If the enemy's defence be
strong and united, send envoys quickly to
him to discover his intention. If he listen

to our advices, he will strike camp and withdraw. But, if he listen not to our advice, but strikes down the messenger, and burns his papers, then divide and attack from five quarters. If victorious, do not pursue; if defeated, flee to a distance. If feigning retreat, proceed slowly, and, if the enemy approach, strike swiftly.

"One army will hold the enemy in front, with another cut his rear, two more with gags in their mouths[2] will attack his weak point, whether on the right or on the left. If five armies thus make alternate onslaughts, success is certain.

"This is the way to strike strength."

And Lord Wen asked and said:

"If the enemy draw near and encompass us, and we would retreat, but there is no way, and in our multitude there is fear, what should be done?"

---

[2] Silently.

And Wu answered and said:

"In such a case, if we be many and they be few, divide and fall upon them; if the enemy be many and we be few, use stratagem and act according to opportunity; and if opportunities be untiringly seized, even if the enemy be many, he will be reduced to subjection."

Lord Wen asked and said:

"If, in a narrow valley with steep places on either side, the enemy be met, and they are many and we are few, what should be done?"

And Wu answered and said:

"If they be met among hills, woods, in deep mountains, or wide fens, advance quickly, retire swiftly, and hesitate not. If the enemy be suddenly met among high mountains or deep valleys, be the first to strike the drum and fall upon them. Let bow and cross bow advance; shoot and capture; observe the state of their ranks;

and, if there be confusion, do not hesitate
to strike."

Lord Wen asked and said:

"If the enemy be suddenly met in a
narrow place with high mountains on either
side, and advance and retreat are alike
impossible, what should be done in such a
case?"

And Wu answered and said:

"This is called war in valleys where
numbers are of no avail. The ablest officers
should be collected, and set against the
enemy. Men light of foot and well armed
should be placed in front; the chariots
divided; the horsemen drawn up, and placed
in ambush on four sides, with many leagues
between, and without showing their weapons.
Then, the enemy will certainly make his
defence firm, and neither advance or retreat.
Whereupon, the standards will be raised,
and the ranks of banners shown, the
mountains left, and camp pitched in the
plain.

"The enemy will then be fearful, and should be challenged by chariot and horse, and allowed no rest.

"This is the method of fighting in valleys."

And Lord Wen asked and said:

"If the enemy be met in a marsh where the water is out, so that the wheels of the chariots sink in, and the shafts be covered, and the chariots and horsemen overcome by the waters, when there are no boats or oars, and it is impossible either to advance or retreat, what should be done in such a case?"

And Wu answered and said:

"This is called water fighting. Chariots and horsemen cannot be used, and they must be put for a time on one side. Go up to the top of a high place, and look out to the four quarters. Then the state of the waters will certainly be seen; their extent, and the deep places and shallows fully ascertained. Then, by stratagem, the enemy may be defeated.

"If the enemy should cross the waters he should be engaged when half over."

And Lord Wen asked and said:

"If there has been long continued rain so that the horses sink, and the chariots cannot move; if the enemy appear from four quarters, and the forces are frightened, what is the course in such a case?"

And Wu answered and said:

"When wet and overcast, the chariots should halt; when fine and dry, they should arise. Seek height, and avoid low places; drive the strong chariots, and choose well the road on which to advance or halt. If the enemy suddenly arise, immediately pursue them."

Lord Wen asked and said:

"If our fields and pastures be suddenly pillaged, and our oxen and sheep taken, what should be done?''

And Wu answered and said:

"Lawless enemies that arise are to be
feared; defend well and do not reply.
When, at sunset, they seek to withdraw,
they will certainly be over-laden and fearful.
Striving to return quickly to their homes,
connection will be lost. Then if they be
pursued and attacked, they can be overthrown.''

Wu the Master said:

"The way of attacking the enemy and
investing his castle is as follows:

"When the outlying buildings have been
taken, and the assaulting parties enter the
innermost sanctuary, make use of the
enemy's officials, and take charge of their
weapons. Let the army on no account fell
trees or enter dwellings, cut the crops, slay
the six domestic animals, or burn the barns;
and show the people that there is no cruel
desire. Those who wish to surrender, should
be received and freed from anxiety.''

VI

ENCOURAGEMENT OF
THE TROOPS

And Lord Wen asked and said:

"If punishment be just and reward
impartial, is victory thereby gained?"

And Wu answered and said:

"I cannot speak of all the things that
concern justice and impartiality, but on
these alone dependence cannot be placed.

"If the people hear the word of command,
or listen to the order with rejoicing; if,
when the army be raised, and a multitude
assembled, they go forth gladly to the fight;
if, in the tumult of the fight, when blade
crosses blade, the soldiers gladly die; upon
these three things can the lord of the people
place his trust."

And Lord Wen said:

"How can this be brought about?"

And Wu answered and said:

"Seek out merit, advance and reward it,
and encourage those without fame."

Accordingly Lord Wen set seats in the
garden of the palace in three rows, and
made a feast unto his chief retainers. In
the first row were set those of chief
merit, and on the table were placed the
best meats and precious utensils. Those
of medium merit were set in the middle
row, and the utensils on the table were
fewer in number. Those without merit
were set in the last row, and utensils of
no value were put before them. And
when the feast was over, and they had all
departed, the parents, wives, and children
of those with merit were given presents
outside the gates of the palace according
to their degree.

Further, messengers were sent yearly
with gifts to condole with the parents of
those who had lost a son in the service of
the state, and to show that they were had
in remembrance.
And after this was carried out for three
years, the people of Chin gathered an army,
and came as far as the Western River.
And when the soldiers of Wei heard this,
without waiting for orders, they armed

themselves and fell upon them; and they
that went forth were 10,000 in number.

And Lord Wen called Wu and said:

"The words that you spoke unto me,
have they not indeed been carried out?"

And Wu answered and said:

"I have heard that there are men, great
and small; souls, grand and feeble.

"As a trial, let 50,000 men, without merit,
be collected, and placed under my command
against the country of Chin. If we fail, the
state will be the laughing-stock among the
princes, and its power under heaven will be
lost. If a desperate robber be hidden in
a wide plain, and 1,000 men be pursuing
him, their glances will be furtive like the
owl, looking backward like the wolf, for
they are in fear of harm from a sudden
onslaught.

"One desperate man can put fear in the
hearts of a thousand. Now, if this host

of 50,000 men become as a desperate thief, and are led against Chin, there is nought to fear.''

On hearing these words Lord Wen agreed, and adding further 500 chariots and 8,000 horse, the hosts of Chin were overthrown, all being due to the encouragement of the troops.

On the day before the battle Wu gave orders to the forces, saying:

''The army will attack the enemy's chariots, horse and foot, in accordance with our commands. If the chariots do not capture the enemy's chariots, or the horse those of the enemy's, or the foot the enemy's footmen, even if their army be overthrown, no merit will be gained.''

Therefore on the day of the battle, the orders were simple, and fear of Wei shook the heavens.

Other Deluxe Classics Available...

With an introduction from Tom Butler-Bowden

- Napoleon Hill
  Think and Grow Rich
  978-1-906465-59-9

- Wallace Wattles
  The Science of Getting Rich
  978-0-85708-008-0

- Niccolò Machiavelli
  The Prince
  978-0-85708-078-3

- Adam Smith
  The Wealth of Nations
  978-0-85708-077-6

- Lao Tzu
  Tao Te Ching
  978-0-85708-311-1

- Plato
  The Republic
  978-0-85708-313-5

Find out more online at www.thisiscapstone.com/classics

CAPSTONE
An Imprint of WILEY
Now you know.